It Takes So Little to Be
ABOVE
AVERAGE

FLORENCE LITTAUER

HARVEST HOUSE
PUBLISHERS
Eugene, Oregon 97402

IT TAKES SO LITTLE TO BE ABOVE AVERAGE

Copyright © 1996 by Harvest House Publishers
Eugene, Oregon 97402

Library of Congress Cataloging-in-Publication Data

Littauer, Florence, 1928–
    It takes so little to be above average / Florence Littauer.—
    Expanded ed.
        p.   cm.
    Includes bibliographical references.
    ISBN 1-56507-397-5 (alk. paper)
    1. Women—Religious life.   2. Women—Conduct of life.
    3. Christian life.   4. Success.   I. Title.
    BV4527.L57   1996   95-34305
    248.8'43—dc20   CIP

Printed in the United States of America.

97 98 99 00 01 02 — 10 9 8 7 6 5 4

Contents

Part IV
It Takes So Little to Understand
Others Above Average

Part V
It Takes So Little to Lead Above Average

Part VI
It Takes So Little to Entertain Above Average

Part VII
It Takes So Little to Care Above Average

Part VIII
It Takes So Little to Pray Above Average

Foreword

In the early seventies, women were crying, "Equality!" and getting into the job market with demands they had never voiced before. Out of necessity, I found myself talking to the vice president of Farmers Insurance Group about becoming an agent. "We don't want women," he said, "but by law, I must give you a chance. If you think you can do a man's job and meet the same requirements, we'll give you the opportunity."

I studied hard, worked late, passed my licensing examination, and met the prerequisites to become a full-line insurance agent. I set my goals for the first year and finished them in nine months. I had proved myself and was no longer on probation.

The production charts showed that our region, which covered a six-state area, had 700 men who were doing an "average job," and that out of that number some were making the "Top Twenty" list. I wanted to make the "Top Twenty" list so I created the motto, "It takes so little to be above average."

I went on to achieve my goal as one of the "Top Twenty" agents and won awards, trips, and walls of plaques. My ultimate accomplishment was receiving the "Distinguished Salesman Award," given to only 33 people in the state of Colorado each year in all sales fields. I attended a banquet at the Hilton ballroom and was presented my trophy by the mayor of Denver. I was no longer average.

A few years later, the Lord led me to sell my successful agency and pursue the calling of Christian writer and speaker. A dear friend had challenged me, saying I had much to share, and I had a burning desire to help hurting women.

I had a purpose but no plan, desire but no delivery, ideas but no image.

After struggling with the fact that I no longer had a professional handle, that my goals were stymied by lack of training, God sent Florence into my life. Two weeks later I flew to Dallas for her sixth Christian Leaders and Speakers Seminar (CLASS). I knew this was what I had been searching for. That week I observed an "above average" woman challenge, motivate, and love 86 women into being "above average."

She taught me to organize my ideas and helped me to set a goal in anything I said or wrote. Because the rewards in the professional world were empty, I had left my career. I pursued what I felt to be God's will for my life, and He has given me a purpose and sent people such as Florence to challenge, encourage, and believe in me.

Florence wrote this book in my home and took my motto as her title. It is our hope that you will be motivated to move in a new direction and be convinced that you are a person of worth who can achieve beyond what you have ever done before. I thank God for Florence as I pursue excellence by following her example. She has proved that in the Christian world it is acceptable to strive, achieve, and be "above average" to God's glory.

You will be challenged in reading this book as you learn that *It takes so little to be above average!*

—Francine Jackson
Evergreen, Colorado

A Note from the Author

As I organized my topics for this book, I pictured a composite woman based on the thousands I had ministered to over the years. I chose subjects that I knew would fit the needs I perceived from my observations. From teaching CLASS, I knew women became excited when they began to think more creatively. I had also learned of the desire for leadership training among Christian women. From my experience in many business meetings, I knew the average chairman was below average. I had observed how few Christians were really "lovers of hospitality" and what an effort it seemed to be to "entertain the saints." I was confident that all of these areas needed to be dealt with in a clear and encouraging manner, and I set out with excitement to write.

Later, as men started coming to CLASS, I saw that many of them, proficient in their careers, also needed to learn to think creatively, to understand the personalities of themselves and others, and to become true partners in home activities. Because of the current pace of family life and the need for many wives to work, it is more imperative than ever for men to become "above average" and not to feel that Father always knows best.

Each brief chapter will benefit both men and women, and I have added a special section for men at the end of each chapter. I have planned 30 challenging subjects so you can each read one a day for a month and hopefully discuss them at dinner. Each subject lends itself well to family discussions and will benefit children as well as adults.

Within one month, using just minutes a day, you can

family that faces each day with confidence and
ıent as you all learn that *"It takes so little to be above*
"

PART I

*It Takes So
Little to Feel
Above Average*

CHAPTER ONE

Pursue Excellence

*S*ome women want to run everything they can get their hands on, and others would rather die than become involved with leadership. Whichever type you are, the day may come when this kind of responsibility falls upon you and you find yourself perilously unprepared. Those who are fearful sometimes become chairmen by a process of elimination and then whimper their way through the year. Even those who love to be up front sometimes hope to run the whole church off the top of their heads.

I went one night to a women's group meeting where the nominating committee chairman stood up and said, "We didn't have time to meet, and so what I thought would be fun would be if we went right around the room and each one of you say why you couldn't be next year's chairman. The one with the worst excuse will be it."

It was my first meeting, and when it got to me, I stated, "I will only be in town for two of the eight meetings." The lady next to me sniffled into her hankie as she cried, "My husband's an atheist, and he'd be furious if he found out I was chairman of any church committee." Other women had extremely creative and colorful excuses. When the vote was taken, the weepy lady and I tied. I pointed out to them how important it is to have a chairman who can be at the meetings, and they released me. Mrs. Weepy became leader by default, and they promised her no one would ever tell her husband she had won.

I left as quickly as I could, dumbfounded at their total lack of parliamentary procedures and grateful the mantle of leadership had been dropped on someone else.

If you were that lady, where would you turn for help? There is no quick school for instant chairmen, but there are some simple steps that can make you above average. It takes so little.

Nobody wants to be average. We don't seek to be ordinary, dull, usual, run-of-the-mill. We would rather be unique, inspiring, significant, above average.

Then why do so many of us trudge down the middle lane of life? Why do we wander through a whole year, rip off the month of December, and wonder what it's all been worth? Why is there always a shortage of leadership in any organization? Or as *Newsweek* asked on its cover, "Where have all the heroes gone?"[1] During the last 30 years of relative affluence, we haven't had to be heroes. We have been able to progress while standing still. We've been able to advance while remaining average. Mediocrity has become accepted as the norm, and people who have tried to excel in any endeavor have been looked upon as odd or pushy. Even the church has been satisfied to accept average as good enough and has labeled the achiever as worldly. Jack Taylor, an above average evangelist and author, says, "Our adversary would divide us by leading us to suppose that aspirations to succeed and humility were enemies; that the Holy Spirit deplores personal motivation; and that positive thinking is an enemy of total commitment."

Don't you sometimes long for a real leader, for a hero who wants to right wrongs, for a heroine who is pure and virtuous? The Bible still asks, "Who can find a virtuous woman? for her price is far above rubies."[2] Yes, who can find a virtuous woman, one who is truly above average?

The late TV anchorwoman, Jessica Savitch, received an honorary degree from Columbia College in Columbia, South Carolina, in June 1983. In challenging the graduates she had said:

> As a reporter, I have had a chance to observe people at the top of just about every field. And it makes no difference if they are male or female, black or white, old or young, the people I observed succeeding are those who have been taught or who teach themselves to strive for excellence. The pleasure comes from knowing you have done a job the best way you know how. It seems to me, however, in our modern society that there is very little done these days in pursuit of excellence. But whatever there is, it stands out for its rarity.[3]

Wouldn't you like to be a rarity, far above rubies? There is such a *need* for leadership today, so many cries for direction. We need women who are willing to say, "Here am I, use me." We need older women to teach the young. We need:

- women who are examples for others to follow
- women who are willing to take a chance
- women who will encourage others
- women who aren't touchy or petty
- women who can think beyond the moment
- women who have the attitude and bearing of
  a leader
- women who try to look their best
- women who can call a meeting to order
- women who will open their homes
- women who have compassion for those in trouble
- women who are ready to pursue excellence

There are so few virtuous women around, so few pursuing excellence in either the world or the average church. Are you willing to read these pages, spend some time on introspection and reflective thinking, and set some new goals?

Because the average of the past has been below average, it is easy for us in the present to aim to be above average in the future.

Let's stand out as a rarity and reach for a crown of rubies.

Additional Challenges for Men:

You may already be above average, but then again you may realize you could have done better. You may see as we progress that you also could learn how to run a meeting more efficiently, how to give and take compliments, how to rise above criticism, how to think in outline form, how to be a caring host, and even how to pray effectively. Although I originally wrote this material to motivate and instruct women, I found that the men who read it asked, "Why didn't you include us?" So in this updated version I've included you.

I'll keep in touch with you as we move along because we do need:

- men who lift up and encourage their wives
- men who are supportive of their wives' activities
- men who don't domineer the family
- men who will be inspirational leaders
- men who will spend time with their children
- men who will dress neatly at home as well as at work
- men who will take part in social planning
- men who are willing to help with housework
- men who realize their wives have talents and gifts
- men who protect their wives from trouble
- men who are truly spiritual leaders

In so many church situations, the men are proclaimed to be the head of the wife without being taught how to be her supporter and cheerleader. You can only lead as far as you have gone, so let's move on together. The basic contents apply to both men and women, but I'll add some special notes for you men as we progress through the book.

So . . . pursue excellence.

It takes so little to be above average.

CHAPTER TWO

Take Aim

W̲e can easily see the demand there is for competent men and women to minister to those in need, but how are they going to be trained, and who is going to train them?

I never cease to be amazed that God has a specific plan for each of our lives and that He knows the beginning from the end. I marvel as I look back over a half-century of experience and see how God has woven my life together and put me in a place of ministry far different from my original plans.

He gave me a British father who instilled in me a love for words and a desire to speak clearly.

He gave me a sensitive mother, a violin and cello teacher, who sent me to elocution lessons because I had "no musical talent."

He allowed me to receive a scholarship to college, where I steeped myself in English literature, apprenticed as a director of musical comedies, and won the title of Best Female Speaker in New England Colleges.

He gave me the ability to teach English and speech on the high school and college level, to direct little theater productions, and to do fashion commentating for Macy's in New York.

He allowed me to be brought to my knees by the births of two hopelessly brain-damaged sons and gave me a genuine compassion for people with problems.

He gave me victory over depression and put me in leadership positions from State Budget Chairman of the League of Women Voters in Connecticut to District Public Speaking Chairman for the Federated Women's Clubs of America.

He allowed my husband, Fred, and me to pull our marriage together and then teach others "how to." He gave me a ministry of motivating, consoling, and inspiring women, and now He has pulled it all together so that I can show others how to give hope to a troubled world.

As I was on a cross-country flight in the fall of 1980, I read a *Vogue* article that said the eighties would be the "Decade of the Active Woman." It predicted that women would be seeking training as never before in whatever courses were available. I wondered what was available and who was going to teach it. When I returned home, I looked in the *Los Angeles Times* calendar section[1] and was amazed at the variety of events planned for that week. Courses were open to the public on:

Psychological Analysis of Zen Meditation
Beginning a New Life Through Simple
    Relaxation
Altruistic Activism: Best Exercise for
    Good Health
Hypnosis: the Key to Your Subconscious Mind

Was *Vogue's* prediction correct? Were people seeking seminars on self-help? The answer came clearly two years later when the *Times* printed a major article, "Americans Take a Long Look Inward": "According to social researchers, 80% of America's adult population is now actively engaged in seeking self-fulfillment. For better or worse, the so-called human potential movement has grown up to become a staple of the culture."[2]

These "crash courses in personal growth" have crashed upon us as waves. So many are coming so fast that one Los Angeles lady has installed a seven-terminal computer system to keep track of the new seminars each week. She publishes a directory of seminars and plans "to start seminars of her own—including seminars for people who want to give seminars."[3]

Suddenly, we have realized we've been treading water, and we want to catch the next wave to success. We want to be above average.

If it's true that 80 percent of the American adult population is seeking self-fulfillment, that figure has to include much of the Christian community. Where are these courses? What are they teaching? Who is doing the instruction?

Such questions led me to a sobering thought. These courses are in the world and of the world, and they are taught by people smart enough to seize an opportunity when they see one. While the church is discussing the color of the new choir robes, its members are running off to worldly courses in hope of finding themselves and becoming relevant.

The "Decade of the Active Woman" has come and gone, but we must continue to provide leadership for the future.

With this need in mind, in the fall of 1980 I invited 40 Christian women to attend a speakers' training seminar in

Redlands, California. These were all women who had the
potential for influential leadership and who only needed the
tools and the motivation. Among those who attended were
four Hollywood personalities who were ready to learn how to
lead for the Lord. Rhonda Fleming, an exquisitely elegant
lady, was motivated to express her faith openly. Since then
she has been on "The 700 Club" twice, has given her testimony to over 1000 women in Minneapolis, has related her
story in *Guideposts*, and has founded a cancer clinic for
women in Los Angeles. The late Bonnie Green, former
showgirl, and husband John Green, the composer and con-
ductor, both appeared on "The 700 Club" and had a ministry
with couples in Beverly Hills. Joanne Dru learned to share
her testimony with others, and Jeanne Cagney, Jimmy's sister, inspired and challenged the audience at the Southern
California Women's Retreat.

God gave these women talent, charm, and personality. He
allowed each one to go through trials and traumas that
brought them to their knees. They had the message of hope
for discouraged women. All they needed were the tools, the
know-how to move out of the wings and onto the stage of life.

As I observed the remarkable changes in the women
during four days of training and the ministries God impressed
upon them as they became equipped, I knew I had to do my
part to fill the leadership gap in the Christian community. I
knew the Lord wanted to use me to lift the levels of
Christian communication. With my husband's encouragement and support, I founded CLASS: Christian Leaders and
Speakers Seminars. In the last 15 years the Lord has used this
instrument to give tools and motivation to over 10,000 men
and women across the country.

He has provided me with a staff of dedicated leaders who

want to teach others to "Say it with CLASS." Some of us plant, some of us water, and God gives the increase.

What about you? Are you ready for God's exciting plan for your life?

It may not take a lot to be above average, but it does take something. It takes desire. Do you care enough to try? It takes a goal. Do you wish to aim high? You've perhaps heard of the airline pilot who announced over the loud-speaker, "I have bad news and good news. The bad news is we're lost and don't know where we're going. The good news is we're making very good time." This simple story represents many of our lives. We're lost, we don't know where we're going, but we're rushing to get there.

Dr. E.V. Hill, the dynamic black evangelist, once challenged a group of leaders at the First Baptist Church in Dallas to "report for duty." He told us that there is a wide gate and a broad way that leads to destruction, and many there are that go down it. But "strait is the gate, and narrow is the way, which leadeth unto life, and few there be that find it."[4] He stated, "It takes no brains to find the broad way. You just waddle out one day, and you're on it. But if you want to find the narrow way, you've got to look for it. You've got to aim for it—and few there be that find it."

There are so many articles and books on motivation that it seems too obvious to mention the importance of setting goals to find the "narrow way." We all know that without a vision the people perish, and that we are to do all things cheerfully as unto the Lord, but sometimes the vision is fuzzy and our cheery turns to dreary.

While we all accept that our first human priority is to care for our families, we should open our minds to the fact that our whole life is a preparation for ministry. For you young women who are at home with children, don't let your mind wander out to pasture. Keep alert, keep reading, keep thinking. Know that God will give you a ministry when He feels you are ready. Don't wait until you can see the hand-writing on the wall; use every available mental moment to prepare today for God's call tomorrow.

One summer when I was teaching drama at Camp Trebor, the archery instructor quit. The director asked if any-one could teach the class. No one volunteered, even though additional wages sweetened the proposition. I did a quick mental review of my college archery class and raised my hand. Even though I had little athletic ability, I remembered the basic principles of the sport, and I lined the young girls up in the field with their bows and arrows. At first we had no target; the girls had to get the arrow moving and learn the basic skills. When they could simply send the shaft sailing somewhere, we set up a target. Up until then they were play-ing games, but they didn't have a goal. It's hard to hit the tar-get when you don't have one. As each girl focused in, she narrowed her aim until she found the target. Some hit the straw around the edge, some scored, and a few found the bull's-eye.

Some of us don't want to practice or prepare until the final target is right before us and we can see the bull's-eye, and yet God often does not reveal His ultimate plan until He sees that we are ready. He doesn't reach down for the idle mind, the lazy body, or the empty spirit. He wants someone who's preparing for the future even when she can't see the target.

Abraham Lincoln was an unlikely candidate for any political office, let alone the presidency of the United States. He was homely, plain, and simple. He did not possess the magnetism or charisma we all want in a leader. Even though he did not look or act like a leader, he prepared for leadership and said, "I'll study and get ready, and then maybe my chance will come."

As I train leaders in CLASS, I find a few who don't want to "waste time" aiming to be above average in case they never get called to lead. But would God waste a prepared person? Especially one who prepared in faith, not knowing the exact goal?

Nina Jean Obel, a lovely Dallas lady with an exceptional home, innate class and breeding, and elegant designer clothes, came to one of our leadership seminars. She took the training not expecting to use it, but wanting to experience all life had to offer. In the eyes of the world she had arrived, and she could rest on her silk damask couch and watch the swans sail by her window. But Nina Jean wanted to be available for the Lord's call whatever that might be, and she came to study. Barbara Bueler was her group leader, and Nina Jean said to her, "I don't know why I'm doing this because I'm really very shy and I don't like to stand up in front of anyone, but I want to be ready."

One morning as Nina Jean sat in a meeting of the Dallas chapter of the Great Commission Prayer Crusade, the ladies were discussing the need to train speakers to meet the demands they had for prayer workshops. No one seemed to know anyone with ability in leadership training and, as the vacuum became more apparent, Nina Jean wondered if this was the place God had in mind for her.

Quietly she raised her hand and told them she had been to CLASS. Within minutes, Nina Jean became the leader of all those who were willing to receive instruction. As she told me this story, she said in amazement, "I can't believe I'm doing this, but I seemed to be the only one who was ready."

Today there are so many opportunities for men and women who are ready. There are so many groups desperate for leaders, so many lonely people craving attention, so many depressed souls waiting for uplifting counsel. Are you ready?

A 96-year-old lady was a faithful attendant at my women's club Bible studies. She came with her lessons prepared and knew all the answers. One day a tactless member asked her, "Why do you work so hard on these lessons when you're so old and it doesn't matter?"

Little Bess Elkins looked up and said confidently, "I'm cramming for my finals."

It's never too late to get ready for our finals. Narrow is the way which leads to life, and few there be that find it. It takes so little to be above average, but it does take a desire to learn. And it does take preparation so when the great target appears, we'll be able to hit the bull's-eye.

In an elegant ad for the sporty and expensive Alfa Romeo, the headline stated, "Now that you've got your act together, take it on the road." I read the copy telling me I could have a car tailored to fit me so well that "You don't just drive it. You practically wear it."

As I considered this thought, I realized how many of us have gone out on the road before we got our act together.

How about you? Make the effort to come in from the highways and byways of life and spend some time in soul-searching and self-improvement. Then when the simple steps and spiritual supplements give you new strength, you'll have your act together and be able to take it on the road, wherever God leads.

Today begin to look toward the goal of being all God made you to be.

ADDITIONAL CHALLENGES FOR MEN:

So much emphasis is put upon goal setting at your workplace that you may not think of priorities at home. Your wife needs you to set goals with her for the family, to plan ahead for time off, for fun times, for vacations. As Hill said, it takes no brains to just waddle through life, but to find the narrow way you have to set goals. Set aside some time to *take aim*. Meet with your children separately and ask them personally about their goals: "What do you want to be? What preparation, schooling, marks do you need to get there?"

One educator told me that in her meetings with parents, they frequently couldn't answer the question, "What is your child's goal in life?" Many said, "He doesn't have one." Yet, when she asked those same parents' children, "What is your dream?" they all had answers. Deep inside, our children have desires. It is our job to sit down quietly where we'll be without distraction and ask them.

So realize your wife needs your support in her dreams, you need your own dreams, and you need to pull the desires out of your children so they will know you care. In these times of negative thinking, it is so important that our children know we are there for them and that the Lord is our hope.

So take aim.

It takes so little to be above average

CHAPTER THREE

Move Up
to Zero

Some people feel they'll never get their act together, that they'll never take it on the road. How about you? Do you think you're below average? Have you grown up feeling insecure? Do you have a low self-image? Do other people always seem smarter or better-looking?

As Christians we don't want a worldly focus on ourselves, yet it is foolish to be held down by an inferiority complex that keeps us from encouraging other people. Many of us feel that since Paul said, "In me is no good thing," we are to live in a constant state of self-flagellation. If anyone compliments us, we feel we should instantly deny the praise and negate any uplifting thought. In David Seamands' book, *Healing for Damaged Emotions*, he corrects the faulty theology that a self-belittling attitude is pleasing to God. He says that this precept of low self-worth being godly

. . . is not true Christian humility and runs counter to some very basic teachings of the

Christian faith. The great commandment is that you love God with all your being. The second commandment is an extension of the first—that you love your neighbor as you love yourself. We do not have two commandments here, but three: to love God, to love yourself, and to love others. I put self second, because Jesus plainly made a proper self-love the basis of a proper love for a neighbor. The term *self-love* has a wrong connotation for some people. Whether you call it self-esteem or self-worth, it is plainly the foundation of Christian love for others. And this is the opposite of what many Christians believe.[1]

When we ask Jesus Christ into our hearts, He promises to come in and give us abundant lives. He adopts us into His family, we become just a little lower than the angels, we are His royal priesthood, we are the temple of His Holy Spirit, and we know when He comes again we will be like Him. We are children of the King, and yet so few of us lay hold of that truth. It's difficult to be above average when our self-image isn't yet up to zero.

A friend of mine was asked to speak to a group of 40 networkers. They met in a home and, when it was time for her part of the program, she explained what they were going to do. "Each one of you turn to the person next to you, who is not your spouse, and give that person three compliments."

As she watched, it was like lights going on all over the room. "I've noticed your big brown eyes. They seem so excited when you talk." "They do? I've never thought my eyes were pretty. My father said blue eyes were better." "They might be for someone else, but brown is just right for you." "Wow, I never thought of that." The group got so inspired lifting each other up that when she tried to bring them back to her message, they begged for more time. At the end they proclaimed it the best evening they'd ever had.

One lady wrote me after our Fort Worth CLASS and poured out her heart: "Over the years when I would attend a funeral, I would wonder what the preacher would have good to say about me. I had let my self-image be pretty low a lot of the time."

Maureen Jordan came to CLASS at the Crystal Cathedral in Southern California and confessed a lifetime of traumas that had left her with an extremely low picture of herself. As the staff ministered to her, she began to look at herself in a new light, unfolding in a radiant manner. Later she wrote:

> CLASS meant so much to me. It was a turning point, a life-changing experience. You have given me *hope* that I can someday share my story in such a way that others may know Jesus Christ and His unconditional love for us all. We don't hear as much of how He restores our broken self-image when we come to Him as I would like. So maybe someday soon I'll be one of His healed helpers.

Are you a little insecure or self-conscious? Are you not quite up to zero? Let's take a self-image inventory. On the next page is a list of physical, mental, and spiritual areas in your life about which you have a ready-made opinion. Read each item and then put down the first descriptive word that comes to your mind. For example, I would write: Looks, plain; Hair, straight; Intellect, smart. Do only this first column now.

SELF-IMAGE

What is it?   The opinion and value you
                         place on yourself, the
                         reflection of your inner
                         real self.

What is the origin? Parents, friends, employers,
                         mates, children, self.

Is your self-image correct? Take this self-analysis.

	Descriptive Word	Origin of Opinion
Looks		
Hair		
Eyes		
Weight and shape		
Posture and bearing		
Clothes		
Sense of style and color		
Self-confidence		
Personality		
Intellect		
Ability to converse		
Knowing current events		
Leadership skills		
Spiritual dedication		
Bible knowledge		
Compassion for others		

After you have written words of self-evaluation, go back
and count how many are positive and how many are negative.

My straight hair and plain looks would both be negatives, and my smart mind would be a plus. If you have more negatives than positives, you obviously do not have a healthy self-image. But we won't leave the matter there. Let's look at the next column.

Read each item and descriptive word again. Think back as far as you can to when you first got that opinion of yourself. Who first gave you that idea? What incident caused you to draw this conclusion about yourself?

I remember an aunt who said to my mother, "Don't worry about Florence being so plain; they all improve as they grow up." When I think back, I know how hurt I was in first grade when I tried out for the part of the rose or even the lily and was chosen as the cowslip. My whole role was to walk heavy-footed across the stage and then fall down in a heap. As I picked myself up, everyone laughed because I had ripped my crepe-paper petals off in the fall. I was so embarrassed and realized I had a "dumb part" because I wasn't pretty. Each spring our church had a May Day celebration, and lovely little girls were chosen to dance delicately around a maypole, weaving streamers in and out. When I volunteered, they asked me to sit on the box to hold the maypole steady. At Christmas I wanted to be Mary, but I didn't try out when the Sunday school teacher said, "Only the pretty girls should come." In high school I wanted a lead in the senior-class play, *The Fighting Littles*. The all-American beauties got the parts, and I had a few lines as Cuckoo, the dingbat.

As you read over the negatives about yourself, think about where you first got these thoughts. Jot down the occasion or the person who planted this concept in your mind.

Now do the same with the positives. I remember so many times when I would be standing next to my little brother Jim and people would say to my mother, "Isn't Jim adorable with his curls!" Then they'd look at me with my straight dutch-cut hair and sigh, "She must be smart." I decided very early in life that I had better get smart. It seemed to be my only asset, so I studied hard. In high school I got on the honor roll, won a scholarship to college, carried three full majors, stayed on the dean's list, and graduated with honors in speech. At least I was smart!

As I have gone over this chart with men and women in seminars, I have learned how consistently the basis for our self-image comes from people and events in our childhood. Perhaps it was a teacher who said, "Why aren't you smart like your sister?" a father who shouted, "You trip over everything!" a mother who sighed, "We've done the best we can with her," a stranger who patted you on the head and said, "You're cute for a fat girl."

Where did our poor self-image come from? Now, what are we going to do with the negative results? It's not enough to *face* the fact that we have some low opinions of ourselves or even to *trace* their origins. We now have to work to *erase* these attitudes. We don't need to carry the burden of thoughtless people from long ago and far away on our backs any longer. By now some of you may have had your eyes opened. You know why you haven't felt secure within yourself. Just this revelation is often a relief.

Does this negative feeling have any sound foundation at this point in my life? Am I dragging a dead horse around the block? Do I need to be worried about straight hair anymore? No. We have permanents, curling irons, and hot rollers at our disposal and, for a change or cover-up, there are wigs and hairpieces. There is hardly a woman alive who can't have curly hair today. Even men can color their hair or fill in the bald spots.

Am I still that plain little girl who lived in three rooms behind a variety store? Am I still in Work Progress Administration dresses that come in three pastel shades? Yes, inside I am. I'm still waiting to play the role of the queen, still wanting to win a beauty contest, still shocked when someone calls me elegant. Do you see how early impressions hang on even when there is conflicting evidence?

Let's get rid of these ridiculous carry-overs today. Let's look at them for what they are: ancient history that we have allowed to drag us down far too long. Go over your list and draw a line right through each negative word that is not valid anymore. You aren't fat or dumb. You don't have beady eyes or a bad complexion.

Paul tells us in Philippians 3:13,14 (RSVB), "One thing I do, forgetting what lies behind and straining forward to what lies ahead, I press on toward the goal for the prize of the upward call of God in Christ Jesus." Cross off your list and erase those unnecessary burdens. Don't let an old aunt who is now dead ruin your self-image. Don't let a third-grade teacher have control over you when you're 30 years of age. Don't let a casual comment tossed lightly years ago hang heavily upon you today.

Anne Thornton came to our first CLASS and filled out this self-image chart. Later she told me this time of introspection had opened up her eyes to some previously unexplained hang-ups. She saw the background reasons for some of her insecurities and realized how ridiculous it was that criticism heard in her childhood was still influencing her opinion of herself today. As she prayerfully worked to overcome these insidious relics of the past, she was able to free her mind from the quiet brooding that had been a resident negative all her life. As she examined and released these old evaluations, she was able to apply these same steps to helping other women in her Bible-study class. Her leadership skills improved as she was able to accept herself as God had made her, not as other people had influenced her to believe.

The next time someone compliments you on one of your touchy areas, thank the person instantly and thank the Lord for this reinforcement and this healing of your image. Now ask the next question.

Is this negative feeling actually a valid problem in my life? If it is, what am I going to do about it?

Francine Jackson, one of our CLASS staff, told me how as a child she was laughed at because she "ran funny." Later people called her gawky and gangly. She was the tallest girl in her high school class, and some said her neck was too long. She tried to pull her head down into her shoulders, and she slumped over when she walked, but she still knew people were staring at her and whispering about her. Her teeth weren't even, so she tried not to smile. Do you see how much effort was going into cover-up activity? "I felt like a turtle," Francine said. "I wanted to pull my head, neck, and limbs inside a shell and hide."

What do you do when you examine yourself and find these evaluations to be at least partly true? Francine began to keep a journal of her feelings. "Lord, I feel awkward, and I want to be graceful. What should I do?" As she put her thoughts on paper, she began to deal with them first in her heart and then in her actions. She decided to stand up straight and be stately. She held her head up high, and her long neck became regal. She bought clothes with collars that stood up and framed her neck, instead of choking it off. She began to walk with confidence. As she worked prayerfully and humanly on her shortcomings, people's comments changed. "You have lovely long legs. . . . What a graceful neck!" "Beautiful posture."

As Francine's self-confidence improved, she dared take on her other problem, and at 37 years of age she had braces put on her teeth. Those have since been taken off, revealing an even, beautiful smile.

What do you do if you think of yourself as fat, and you are? What do you do if you feel you dress poorly, and you do? What if your teenager says your glasses frames are old-fashioned, and they are? What if your friends get mad because you're always late, and you are? What if your husband says you don't know what's going on in the world, and you don't? What if your wife complains you never come home on time, and you don't?

Do you see how easy it is to come up with answers to these hypothetical questions? But what are you going to do about the real ones?

After listening to my tape on "Marriage Preservation," Liz Page realized her knowledge of the news was limited. She decided to take action and she wrote me: "I made a date with my husband to watch the ten o'clock news. A feminine bathrobe, two glasses of cider, and a willingness to discuss the news made for a happy husband. Thanks for the nudge!"

We all need to be nudged into action in some area of our lives. Let's review our concerns and some possible cures. You've written down descriptive words about yourself. You've counted up the negatives, and you've looked back in your life to see where you first got these ideas. You've asked yourself whether there is any validity in these opinions in the light of today. When you thought about these attitudes, you realized how ridiculous they were, and you crossed them off the page and prayed them out of your mind.

Now look at the leftovers—problems that still need solutions. List them on the lines below. What kind of action should you take? Do you need to lose weight? Update your hair, makeup, glasses frames? Listen to the news and read a few books? Get yourself on a schedule? Think over these areas where you have a negative self-image, and then plan some action you can take. It's so easy to sit around in the ashes of self-pity waiting for a fairy godmother to transform us, but let's not allow our insecurities to become cover-ups for laziness or excuses for inaction. You do the possible, and let God do the impossible.

Concerns   Action

_____   _____

_____   _____

_____   _____

This action list becomes your new set of goals. Are there some things left that you can't do much about at the moment? Do they need *more space*—a special area for you to read or study, a closet for off-season clothes, a playroom for the children; *more money*—redecorating the living room, updating your wardrobe, getting your teeth straightened; *more time*—doing some home baking, altering your clothes, enrolling in a college course, writing the great American novel?

Write down these concerns, hopes, and dreams, giving yourself some suggestions on what future action you could take. This list becomes your long-range goals.

Concerns   Future Action

_____   _____

_____   _____

_____   _____

What negatives are still on your list? Are there some things left that, short of plastic surgery or a new brain, you can't do anything about (you have short legs, you can't write poetry, or you look just like your least-favorite aunt)? Write down these thoughts that have troubled you.

Concerns   Acceptance

_____   _____

_____   _____

_____   _____

Read them objectively and laugh at how petty these problems really are. Ask the Lord to help you accept yourself as you are, knowing that not one of us is perfect, and so many other people are in extremely trying situations.

At our CLASS in Tampa we had a beautiful lady attend in a wheelchair. She had cancer, and her leg had been amputated to the hip. She had an artificial limb which was extremely uncomfortable, and she was in constant pain. In spite of this, she stood up when it was her turn to introduce herself, and she smiled bravely as tears came down her cheeks. She participated in each activity and was gracious to everyone who spoke with her. By the end of the three days together, the other women realized how trivial many of their problems were. You could not complain that God didn't give you two lovely legs when you observed the strength of a lady who had only one.

Review the concerns you wrote down. Do they really matter? As you check off God's acceptance of you, begin to accept yourself as you are.

So many women come to me with weight problems that have become such burdens to them that the concerns are usurping control of their actions and personalities. Some have supposedly tried every diet in the world and can't lose an ounce. They've bought every diet book and gone to every health seminar, and nothing has helped. I know one woman who has three lifetime memberships in health clubs and only has "guilt over not going" as her result. Many women talk endlessly about their diets and defeats, making themselves not only overweight but boring.

What do you do if you can't overcome a problem and you have sincerely tried? You accept the situation and say, "Dear Lord, You know I don't want to be this way. I have tried to eliminate this area of my life, and it's still here. Help me to accept myself as I am and not ruin my whole life over one problem. I know You made me and love me and don't want me harping on this subject any longer. When You are ready, lead me to victory."

A lovely young girl came up to me recently and told me she had listened to me speak when I used Philippians 4:11: "I have learned, in whatsoever state I am, therewith to be content." I had asked the audience to think of things that they were upset over and not content about. She realized that she was set on having a baby and, after eight years of marriage, could not get pregnant, regardless of tests, vitamins, exercise, minor surgery, and prayer.

That day, at my suggestion, she gave up her obsession over having a baby and asked the Lord to make her content without being a mother. She told her husband of her decision to be content, and he was relieved. She had not realized that her constant talk about babies had made him feel insecure and inadequate. They both agreed to stop concentrating on this one problem in life and focus on what was good in their marriage. As they accepted their situation as it was,

they began to relax. She had not known how much emotional energy she was using in this intense concentration on
reproduction. Three weeks after her decision to be content,
she got pregnant. She was so excited to tell me the news,
and she added, "Keep telling women to accept their situations and learn to be content. God works much quicker in
an accepting and relaxed human being."

God grant me the serenity to accept the things
I cannot change; courage to change the things I
can; and wisdom to know the difference.

—Reinhold Niebuhr

Carol Kent, CLASS graduate from Michigan, gives her
testimony on self-image. She recalls the day in grammar
school when the little boys were laughing at her, and she
heard one say, "You're right, she does have big lips." She
went home crying and tried to come up with ways to "pull
in" her lips. She grew up fearful that friends would make fun
of her lips, and some did. Here was something she couldn't
do anything about. As she matured, she learned to accept
the looks God had given her. Instead of sitting tight-lipped
in a corner, Carol (now an author) has been on many TV
talk shows and has appeared on the cover of *Today's
Christian Woman*. How about you? Can you throw away the
incorrect assessments you've had of yourself? Are you willing
to change areas that really need improvement? God says you
are acceptable unto Him just the way you are, so don't let
the past ruin your future.

Today look at yourself in the mirror and see what a wonder God has created.

ADDITIONAL CHALLENGES FOR MEN:

I frequently have women tell me that when they try to get their husbands to do a communication exercise such as we have suggested in this chapter, they say it's stupid or childish or just for women. Yet men need to spend time in meaningful conversation with the family. This type of family discussions is not "stupid"—it is vital to the feeling of being a unit, of being a family whose members care about each other.

Over the years I have received many exciting comments from men who sat down and reminisced about how they felt as children. Now their own young ones relate to them in a new way and accept their father as a real human being. Be willing to fill out the chart on how you felt about your looks, your personality, and your ability to converse as a teenager. Share these feelings with your children. Help them write down their concerns, the things they wish were different. Then talk about the action it would take to change the situations. No matter what they come up with, don't say it's a dumb idea. Listen, help, and affirm.

A business executive told me, "The biggest problem I have with my employees is their total lack of self-worth. They've been told they can't make it, and they've believed the lie. It seems to be too late to change their opinion."

Wouldn't it be great if you could be the vehicle to change your children's self-image before their feelings become lifetime habits? Find out where they seem to be insecure and help them get over these areas. Start today by using the questions and plans in this chapter. The lives you change by your willingness to spend time may be your own children's.

Move up to zero.

It takes so little to be above average.

CHAPTER FOUR

Bring Out the Best

Anxiety in a man's heart weighs him down, but a good word makes him glad.
—Proverbs 12:25 (RSVB)

*A*s I was speaking on depression in a Texas town, I asked how many could remember a specific childhood incident when someone had said something that really hurt, something that stamped a deep negative impression onto the mind. Almost every hand went up. I asked those willing to share to stand up, and many told of past experiences that were still real in their minds today.

One lady remembered how her father wanted a boy and how he had frequently said, "You'd have been all right if you'd been a boy." One girl told of the teacher who often asked her, "How did you ever get into the gifted program? You sure don't belong here." One woman in elegant and expensive clothes came up after the lecture and confessed, "I've been verbally abusing my two children, and I didn't realize it until today."

When we look objectively at others and listen to their pain, we can see how thoughtless comments made to children have lasting, damaging results. Lately, we have heard so much about anorexia nervosa, an ailment where the victim literally starves to death. The sufferer is usually a young woman obsessed with having a slim body. Any obsession is abnormal, but this one leads to a critical body condition. Why do girls starve themselves? Why do they still diet when they have lost 40 percent of their body weight? Dr. Jean Mayer gives this answer:

> Obviously, anorexia nervosa does not begin with compulsive dieting. A psychological history often shows that the girl was chubby or downright fat, and that the drive to start dieting had been triggered by a disparaging remark about weight from someone whose opinion was highly valued, usually an older man.[1]

What damage a "disparaging remark" can cause! We must realize the power each one of us has in the tongue. We can use our words to build up, or we can use them to tear down. A leader should encourage others. A leader must give hope.

In Proverbs 25:11 it says, "A word fitly spoken is like apples of gold in pictures of silver." We use this verse as our CLASS motto, aiming to be clear, constructive, and complimentary in every word we say. Ephesians 4:29 is a verse we had our whole family memorize: "Let no corrupt communication proceed out of your mouth, but that which is good to the use of edifying, that it may minister grace unto the hearers."

How simple it sounds to say only those words which will edify and build up the listener. How we would like each one of our words to minister grace or do a favor for the hearer. One day I was attending a church service and was asked on the spot to give a children's sermon. I stood before rows of young people and taught them Ephesians 4:29 from memory. As I broke it into parts, I asked, "What does it mean to 'minister grace'?"

A little girl stood up and said proudly, "Grace is God's unwarranted favor." I was thrilled. I had a spiritual giant on my hands.

"What does that mean?" I asked.

"I have no idea," she responded sadly.

"Where did you learn it?"

"In Sunday school," she answered, "but the teacher didn't tell us what it meant."

I wondered how may lessons I had taught children that sounded good but had no practical application.

I explained that she was right in her definition, and that grace meant to do a favor, to give out a gift.

"Oh," she replied, "like giving someone a present full of good words!" She was excited over her creative idea.

I loved her simple concept and asked the children to think of their conversations as opportunities to give presents to their friends. "From now on, when you open your mouth, picture each word as a little gift, wrapped up in pretty paper with a bow on top."

I then reviewed the whole verse—that our words should be good and not bad, they should build people up and not knock them down, they should minister grace (do a favor, be like a gift). As I concluded, another little girl jumped out into the aisle, turned to the audience, and stated clearly, "What she means is our words should be like a little silver box with a bow on top!"

The whole congregation gave a collective "oh." What an idea that our words should be gifts—little silver boxes with bows on top!

How many of us mothers when our children take that first look at us in the morning (which could be a frightening experience in itself) hear them say, "There's Mother. Wait till she opens her mouth, and out will tumble little verbal gifts?" Do they stand with a basket and beg, "More words, Mother—more silver boxes with bows on top?" Do they bring their friends home and say, "Wait till you meet my mother. Every word she says is precious, like a present. Around here it's like Christmas every day."

How about you? Are your words presents? When you speak to your child, your parent, or your mate, do you do them a favor? Perhaps you should put little silver boxes in each room in your house to remind you that your words are to be like gifts. It takes no time, trouble, or thought to be critical. It just comes naturally, but oh, how it can hurt!

In a recent seminar, Dr. William Glasser was heard to say that over 90 percent of all breakups in human relationships are because of criticism. We hate to receive it, but we seem to enjoy dishing it out, breaking the spirit of those around us.

> A merry heart doeth good like a medicine: but a broken spirit drieth the bones.
> —Proverbs 17:22

> Pleasant words are as an honeycomb, sweet to the soul, and health to the bones.
> —Proverbs 16:24

Could you make a commitment today to cease criticizing others and drying up people's bones? Could you make a prayerful effort to use pleasant words sweet to the soul?

Could you become a traveling physician dispensing pieces of your merry heart, doing good like a medicine?

Bonnie Green was telling our CLASS about several visits she had made to the home of Joe and Rose Kennedy. I asked her, "What was there about that family that turned out so many leaders?"

She replied, "It was because the father and mother encouraged their children to greatness." She told of a certain night when she was 20 and insecure. She sat at the dinner table, and Father Kennedy asked her a political question beyond her ability to answer. She pulled the best thought she could from her resources and made a statement. As she finished, Mr. Kennedy looked her straight in the eye and said, "That was a brilliant answer. May I quote you on this?" Bonnie never forgot that moment *he* wanted to quote *her*! "The Kennedys had the ability to *bring out the best* in others."

How I want to be that kind of person—not one who dries up the bones, but one who brings out the best in others. We don't stop to realize the harm we can do with our words. But as we review how others have hurt our self-image in the past, we want to be careful that we aren't doing the same thing. I have learned from available statistics that we tend to repeat the mistakes of our parents. For example, a boy who was beaten by his father, hated every minute of mistreatment, and vowed he would never lay a hand on his son, grows up to beat his child. Our intellect tells us not to do these negative things, but when we are in a stressful situation, we react emotionally as our parents did in the same set of circumstances. We don't map out our feelings, we just react instantly.

If we were told as children we were dummies, we tend to pass this on to our children. Isn't it time to break the chain?

Bill Glass, who is involved in prison ministry, asked a group of inmates how many had parents who had told them that they were stupid and would end up in jail? One hundred percent raised their hands in affirmation. What does this story teach us? That the words and attitudes we put into our children is what they will reproduce. We plant seeds today that will become the flowers or weeds of tomorrow. Currently we hear much about computers, and we know that these instruments can produce no information that has not been put in: "Garbage in, garbage out." If you feed it negative material, it will spew out negative answers.

Look at the mind of your child as a little computer. What material are you feeding into it? What caustic comments from you will create an inferiority complex in your child? We are programming these computers for their future reactions. Are you laying the foundation for a creative mind or for a critical tongue? What they hear now is what they'll say later.

There is one whose rash words are like sword thrusts, but the tongue of the wise brings healing.
                                        —Proverbs 12:18 (RSVB)

When my daughter Marita was 18 and in a rebellious stage, I determined to pour my life into her in such a way that she would want to stay in the fold. I told her daily how much I loved her and what a joy she was to my life. I did not criticize her clothes or companions, and I made all her friends welcome in our home. I took her with me on speaking trips and, while she appeared disinterested in what I was teaching, the words were going into her computer. She liked the excitement of traveling, and she accepted "listening to Mother" as paying her way.

Once I said to her, " I can envision the two of us speaking together: you doing outer beauty and me doing inner beauty." Years later she reminded me of my statement and let me know what her reaction had been at the time. She had made no comment then but had said to herself, "That will be the day when I spend my time in churches with women!"

We continued to spend our time in churches with women. Marita listened to my speaking, Bible teaching, and counseling. At the end of each day I would go over the life stories of the different women and ask her what she thought each should do to overcome her problems. Whatever she came up with as an answer, I would compliment her on her sound thinking.

One day she announced, "I want to travel with you all the time. What should I do to get ready?" Marita had always had an eye for color. Her college courses were in design, and she had become a sharp and stylish dresser. We found customized training for her, and she became a color consultant. When I was asked to speak at women's retreats, I would volunteer Marita as a special feature on fashion, and they would be glad to get a free bonus. As she spoke to women, I would evaluate her performance. She had a teachable spirit, and soon her ability moved from adequate to above average.

When she was 20 and in business for herself, Marita told me, "When I'm doing color consultations with ladies, they start telling me their marriage problems, and I'm just amazed at the answers I give them. I've never been married, and yet I open my mouth and out comes the right advice. Then I realize it's your words, Mother, that I'm saying. It's my mouth, but it's your advice. Those years of filling me up have paid off."

How grateful I am that Marita has stored up more information from her Christian mother than from atheistic professors. The Bible tells us that when we as "virtuous women" have done what we should do, our children will rise up and call us blessed (Proverbs 31:28). Marita has chosen to follow in my footsteps, and that is blessing enough for me.

Marita is in her thirties now and married. She speaks at churches, businesses, and writers' conferences, and is the director of marketing for CLASS. She has even followed in my footsteps by writing four books, even though she had no interest in writing high school compositions.

Never underestimate the power you have to program the computer mind in your child. What you put in will later come out. One day when Fred and I took our nine-year-old grandson Bryan out shopping, we drove into the Wal-Mart parking lot. Bryan spoke up. "We should not trade in Wal-Mart. They come into towns, sell at low prices, and put others out of business. It's not fair to the small businessman who's working hard to make a living." Where did this little speech come from? Was he reading the *Wall Street Journal,* or did he hear his father and mother talking about the effects of Wal-Mart on their small business? We may not ever know they're listening because they don't seem to hang on our every word. They don't even want us to know they've heard what we've said, but *they have.* Keep feeding the machine.

> *Train up a child in the way he should go: and when he is old, he will not depart from it.*
> —Proverbs 22:6

How much of what goes into your child's mind comes from you? How much comes from the mother down the street? From a babysitter? From friends? From teachers? From television?

Today begin to fill your child with positive information and verbal gifts.

ADDITIONAL CHALLENGES FOR MEN:

The Bible tells us we are responsible for training our children diligently when we walk or sit and even when we lie down and rise up (Deuteronomy 6:7). That's *all the time!* What are you doing with your children? Are you critical or complimentary? Do you lift up or knock down? Do you bring out the best or the worst?

In a eulogy to the late Paul "Bear" Bryant, famous Alabama football coach, *Newsweek* (February 7, 1983) said that he:

> . . . always held some secret or strategy or win-
> ning edge that nobody quite figured out . . . . It's
> hard to guess whether the Bear would rather be
> remembered for the god-like image or the human
> virtues. Come to think of it, he would probably
> approach the problem the way he did the rest of
> football and life. He'd settle for the best of every-
> thing.

Truly, Bear Bryant with 323 wins was "the best," and he brought out the best of everything in others. Why don't you practice bringing out the best in others? If you want your child to be above average, check the quality of the material you're putting into his brain. He can't give out anything better than the accumulation of what has gone in. Feed him frequently, nourish him well, for what goes in today is what will come out tomorrow.

What do your children hear you say? Do you swear but punish them for swearing? Do you tell them Sunday school is good for them but stay home yourself? Do you belittle their mother and criticize the food? Do you ask why their B's couldn't be A's?

When I talk with troubled adults, far more tell me they were hurt by their father's words than by their mother's. Many say their fathers did nothing but criticize and complain. "We knew we could never please him, so after a while we quit trying."

In business if you picked on your employees and criticized them constantly, they would all quit, but your children can't quit. They have an 18-year sentence. Think of how you felt when your father said you were too skinny or too dumb. How did you feel when he called you a sissy because you cried? Take a moment to reflect on your childhood verbal pain, and then determine that you will say words that build up and don't knock down, that do a favor like a gift, like a little silver box with a bow on top.

Bring out the best in others.

It takes so little to be above average

CHAPTER FIVE

Accept the Best

Not one of us wants to be criticized, yet we seem equally uncomfortable with praise. Some of us have been knocked down so long that we don't feel we deserve a compliment, and some of us doubt that any positive person is really telling the truth. Where does this negative attitude place the positive person? How does this kind and uplifting individual feel when he has given a compliment and the recipient's response ranges from uneasy silence to vehement denial?

How would I feel if I saw you in a royal-purple gown at the president's reception and said, "What a beautiful gown. You look like a queen in purple!" and you returned, "Look like a queen? Are you crazy? I look more like the maid"? You have now let me know I'm stupid and wouldn't know a queen if I were standing in Buckingham Palace.

How about a hypothetical compliment: "That's a lovely linen suit you're wearing today." Some possible responses: "This old thing?" "This isn't linen; it's just rayon." "I picked it up at Goodwill." "It's a reject from my sister."

Any of these comments show I have no taste and remind me never to say a nice word to you again.

Many ladies complain that their husbands never give them compliments. One man summed it up when he said, "I used to tell her how good she looked, and she'd always make me feel like a dummy for saying so. Finally, I quit noticing anything, and now she complains."

A dentist complimented his receptionist, "Your hair looks great today."

She retorted, "What was wrong with it yesterday?"

We mean to be humble, but we insult the intelligence of the givers when we refuse their compliments. How much happier we can make others when we express gratitude for their comments. A simple "Thank you" is sufficient, but if you wish to make a positive addition, that is even better:

"Your hair always looks attractive."
"Thank you. I'm really pleased with my hair-dresser at Plaza Place."

"I love your black dress."
"Thank you. My husband picked it out especially for this occasion."

"Your new outfit is the latest style."
"Thank you. Coming from someone with your taste, I especially appreciate your comment."

"You play the piano beautifully."
"Thank you. My years of practice have finally paid off."

Accept each compliment as you would a present, words wrapped up in a silver box with a bow on top. Say "Thank you," and you'll receive more; reject the praise, and you'll soon receive none.

Today bless the giver by accepting the compliment graciously.

ADDITIONAL CHALLENGES FOR MEN:

Men seem to be able to accept compliments at work more than they can in personal or family situations. One young woman told me, "Anytime we gave my father a compliment, he'd snap back, 'What are you trying to get out of me now?' We were just being nice, but he couldn't accept it. So after a while we stopped praising him for anything, and he called us ungrateful."

Unfortunately, this same woman seemed unable to say a kind word to her husband, who was longing for a loving phrase. What her father had refused to give to her, she could no longer give to others.

If your children say anything positive to you, stop and thank them. If possible, make a positive conversation out of their compliment. "Thank you for noticing my tie. I'm glad you like it. Your mother gave it to me for Christmas. What do you like best about choosing presents for others? Do you always buy things you like yourself?"

When you listen to your children, thank them, and then involve them in a positive exchange, they will enjoy having you around. Receive your compliments like a gift.

Accept the best.

It takes so little to be above average.

CHAPTER SIX

Accept the Worst

*N*ow that we are all able to accept compliments, what should we do about accepting criticism? Not one of us loves to hear what's wrong with us; no normal person looks to be hurt. We all wish our friends and family loved us unconditionally, as they should, but we are all realistic enough to know that many people feel led to give us some "constructive criticism." Proverbs 12:16 (TLB) says, "A fool is quick-tempered; but a wise man stays cool when insulted." Ignoring an insult is easier said than done. How can we learn to handle harsh words?

Since I always teach from my own experiences, let me share how I developed a plan for accepting the worst. As I analyzed my dislike for negative evaluations, I determined I would *learn to "take it."* I would grit my teeth and accept whatever was dumped on me. This "keep your mouth shut" attitude kept me out of trouble, but it didn't calm my turbulent insides. The more active I became in the speaking world, the more criticism I received. I became a believer of

James' statement, "Let not many of you become teachers . . . for you know that we who teach shall be judged with greater strictness" (James 3:1 RSVB). I decided "taking it" wasn't enough; I had to take it cheerfully. As I prayed about the ability to do this, the Lord showed me I had to *be thankful for each comment.* You mean, say thank you for criticism?

Let's think about this possibility. What does the person who gives you unsolicited advice expect from you? He expects you will become defensive, lose your Christian cool, and therefore validate his opinion that you have a problem and aren't practicing what you preach. Since you don't want to give him this affirmation of his evaluation, accept his advice cheerfully and thank him for it. This stops him in his tracks in a most positive way and prevents him from proceeding to points B, C, and D.

In pursuing this plan, I have developed some helpful answers where I don't have to resort to lying. I may not think much of the idea, but I can always say, "Thank you for sharing that thought with me"; "Thank you for the time you put into this analysis"; "Thank you for caring enough to point that out"; "I appreciate your thoughts, and I will surely discuss them with the staff"; "I must say, I have never considered that before, but I will give your suggestion some thought."

All of these comments are positive and true and will deal with the critic cheerfully. As you become good at accepting criticism and develop your own style of response, you can then move on to the third step: *Ask for it.* That step is the graduate work in our Christian living. We feel we've made progress when we can first take it, then take it cheerfully. But when the Lord is really in control of our lives, He will prompt us to ask for it. So often in Proverbs it says that a wise man asks for counsel, while a fool despises instruction, and that if you rebuke a wise man he will love you, but a fool will hate you. If a wise man loves rebuke and I want to be wise, I must look for helpful suggestions. I must ask for evaluation. How could I have done even better?

As I perceived this plan as a path to wisdom, my defensive attitude disappeared and I developed a spiritual willingness to seek counsel. I don't want to be one of Solomon's fools. Indeed, "Better is a poor and a wise child than an old and foolish king, who will no more be admonished" (Ecclesiastes 4:13).

So ask yourself three questions:

1. Are you willing to take criticism?
2. Are you willing to take it cheerfully?
3. Are you willing to ask for it?

Let's assume you wish to be wise and not foolish. What should you do when you receive a critical comment, admonishing advice, or a scathing scenario? First, you swallow hard and take it. Then you smile, if possible, and instead of defending yourself, thank the person for caring enough to share these thoughts with you. Let him know you will take these ideas to heart and give them consideration. If you're ready for graduate work, ask for some further help or suggestions.

Now that you've passed your finals, what do you do with this new information? You run it through the "fact filter" in your mind: If it's wise, true, and applicable, act upon it. If it's foolish, false, and ridiculous, forget it. How do you know the difference? Ask the Lord to guide you. If when you test, "Am I sarcastic?" some clear examples come to your mind, you should accept this possibility and work prayerfully to overcome your tendency to make humor at others' expense. If someone says, "You'd look a lot better if you would smile once in a while," ask a close friend if you need to smile more. If she hesitates in answering, you'll know this is a problem you need to work on.

What if you sift it through the "fact filter" and it makes no sense at all? You say, "Lord, if this thought is as foolish as it appears to be, help me to forget it."

> *A wise man's heart discerneth both time and judgment.*
> —Ecclesiastes 8:5

After speaking at a retreat of 3000 women in Michigan, I received a large envelope with the audience evaluations of my performance. I read each one and found the majority to be extremely positive. Several mentioned that the second half of a skit I had produced was too long. I listened to that tape with this thought in mind, and agreed it was too long. I profited from these comments and improved the product.

One lady wrote, "Florence was unexpectedly exciting, which goes to show appearances are deceiving." When I ran this through my mind, I came up confused. I was glad I was exciting, but I wasn't sure what had been deceptive about my appearance. I'll never know, but I surely shouldn't waste much time brooding over this evaluation.

Let's learn to accept suggestions and even insults cheerfully. Let's ask for evaluations and listen thankfully. Let's run them through our mental "fact filter." If they're valid, let's act upon them. If they're of no consequence, let's forget them.

Former Chief Justice Charles Evans Hughes once said, "If you can accept and profit by criticism, you have a priceless ability possessed by few of your fellow men."

Patsy Clairmont is an exceptional communicator and gifted humorist. When she was first on our CLASS staff, she was weak and in poor health. We were all concerned about her, and it fell upon me to make some suggestions. Her initial reaction was defensive as is natural, but the next evening when I went to my hotel room there was a note on my pillow. "Thank you for caring enough about my health to make suggestions." Through these suggestions she was put on a positive program which has led her up the long road to improved physical strength and stamina. She is now an energetic and dynamic speaker and the author of three best-selling books.

When we can accept and profit from what we didn't want to hear, we do have a priceless ability possessed by few.

Today practice smiling when less-than-positive statements are made about you.

ADDITIONAL CHALLENGES FOR MEN:

Many families shudder at the very thought of giving Dad a word of suggestion. "What he says goes, no matter what we think." "He'd kill us if we disagreed." "I'd never take the chance of correcting him, even when I know he's wrong." "Are you crazy?" These are answers I got when I asked teenagers if they felt free to share with their father and give suggestions.

Why is it that men can't handle a critical comment or even a needed correction? Is it the male ego needing to be right? Does "taking it" seem a sign of weakness? Do men just like to fight?

Are you strong enough to take your children one at a time and ask each one what they perceive you could do better in the family setting? If you are really brave, you could do what Fred did and ask for family evaluations. Each New Year's Day we all wrote down what we liked best about each family member and then the area in which each person needed to improve. Fred tallied them up and read back what we thought of each other. It was a major learning experience for all of us. Let your family know you are open-minded and will listen without getting angry.

Accept the worst . . . cheerfully.

It takes so little to be above average.

CHAPTER SEVEN

Win the Blue Ribbon

I've always wanted to be a winner! Many years ago as I was raising my children, I also raised roses. I entered cuttings in the Women's Club Flower Show and won. What does it take for a rose to be a winner? It doesn't just sit there on its slim stem in the sun and excel. It needs care, and sometimes this hurts.

One day I went to a pruning demonstration at Flowerland and learned some basic principles which I remember clearly today:

1. The purpose of pruning is to improve the quality of the roses, not to hurt the bush.

2. Pruning should not be started until the gardener has a clear picture in mind of what he wants the finished product to look like. Since the aim is to make the branches form the shape of an urn, everything should be removed that does not conform to the ultimate plan.

3. Cut off all branches and twigs that stick out

sideways and do not enhance the urn-like shape.

4. Prune out branches in the center that are rubbing against each other, that are at cross-purposes, that are choking out the air.

5. Clip closely any sucker shoots that are growing wildly and sapping the energy from the plant.

6. Make sure your shears are sharp so you won't tear up the branches as you cut them.

As I was preparing a CLASS lesson on being able to take criticism, this whole pruning demonstration came to mind. In John 15 we are told that Jesus is the Vine, we are the branches, and God is the Gardener. He prunes off every branch that doesn't bear fruit, and He prunes each one that does so that it will bear more. Suddenly, I saw a comparison. Picture yourself as a rosebush. You have produced flowers in the past, but God the Gardener knows you could blossom even more. To make you bloom to your full potential, to make you a blue-ribbon winner, He must prune off all that's keeping you from the prize. Let's review the pruning principles and see how they relate to us:

1. Pruning is not punishment but purposeful planning. God is not cutting you to hurt you, but to produce perfection.

2. God the Gardener already has in mind what He wants you to look like. He has a plan for your ultimate use, and only He has the picture of the finished product. When you get rebuffed in one area, stopped in one pursuit, cut by a friend, God knows it hurts, but He knows it is necessary to bring you into His purposeful planning, to shape you like that open vessel.

3. When God, who holds the blueprint, gazes down upon us, He sees branches that are sticking out with no rhyme or reason, pursuits in our life that are without eternal value, selfish goals that detract from our spiritual shape. He needs to cut these off. But since He doesn't stroll around our garden with big pruning shears, He sends people to do it for Him, friends who tell us things "for our own good," mates who point out how much time we're wasting, mothers-in-law who show us how they did it better. Some bushes don't take this pruning kindly, and they never bear much fruit. Some accept the cuts, learn from the comments, and go on to win the prize.

4. Since God's purpose is to produce an open vessel ready to be filled with His Holy Spirit, He needs to empty out all that's cluttering up our lives. He sees branches that are rubbing against each other, causing friction in our relationships, and He has to clip them out. He sees activities that are at cross-purposes, keeping us busy in all directions but achieving little. He sees projects that are positive but are pulling us away from His plan. He sees anger, bitterness, jealousy, and other negative emotions which are choking out our spiritual air so we are gasping for breath. He sends His saints with His scissors to shape us up, and sometimes we refuse to be shorn.

5. Have you ever watched a sucker shoot grow? Recently I had one that touched the roof. One week it wasn't there, and the next week it was ten feet high. It shot off in a flash, using up every ounce of strength the poor bush had. Healthy leaves shriveled up, and buds drooped their little heads. Often we beautiful rosebushes

allow sucker shoots to run rampant. We have projects, problems, or pressures that take over our lives, grow out of control, and drain our energy dry. Unpruned, these shoots so sap our strength that we have no stamina left. God the Gardener knows a sucker shoot when He sees one, and He sends His angels to warn us that we're springing off in the wrong direction, that we need to call a quick halt to this unproductive growth.

6. As God trains His little helpers who come to clip us, He asks them to use sharp shears so we won't be torn up in the process of pruning. However, as with every profession in life, some people are slow learners and inflict more pain than others. But once we accept God's program— *Pruning is not punishment but purposeful planning*—we can absorb the cutting cheerfully and ultimately ask for it.

Do you want your roses to win the prize? Take a moment to evaluate your own life and ask yourself if each principle has become your way of thinking:

1. Know that pruning is for a purpose and that the sooner you accept it, the less it will hurt.

2. Know that God has a visual plan for your life. He can picture what you'll look like when He has brought you into full bloom. He's pruning you to conform you to His image.

3. Know that if God wants to use you in a special way, He will send gardeners to cut off those wasted projects, to tone down your harsh words, to improve your looks. Don't fight off the critics; listen and learn.

4. Know that God sees what's inside you. He grieves that you're bickering with your children and carrying on

a conflict for control with your spouse. He wants to sort out your cluttered mind and blow away the chaff. He pleads with you to empty out your bitterness and strife and let Him fill you with His Spirit and His love, joy, peace, patience, kindness, goodness, faithfulness, humility, and self-control (Galatians 5:22,23).

5. Know that each one of us has a sucker shoot at one time or another and ask yourself what it is that's draining strength from your life. If you can cut it off yourself before the Gardener gets there, it won't hurt so much. Do you spend too much time at church and too little at home? Are you exhausted by five o'clock each day and disagreeable at dinner? Are your projects and philanthropies more show than substance? What's your sucker shoot? Self-pruning is painless if you do it quickly.

6. Know that not all pruners have been sent by God; some people go into this business on their own. Listen to their words, run them through your "fact finder," and let God say, "Right on" or "Ridiculous."

When God sends His workers, they will be there not for punishment but for purposeful planning. So the next time you look up and see that lady approaching who loves to cut you down, smile cheerfully, ask for her advice, and pray that her shears are sharp.

Today take a godly view of yourself and look for any sucker shoots that need to be pruned off.

ADDITIONAL CHALLENGES FOR MEN:

If you've ever done any gardening, you know that pruning is not punishment but purposeful planning. You also know in business that the quickest cut is the kindest cut. The sooner you know what you're doing wrong, the sooner you can change and improve. I thoroughly enjoy speaking to businessmen because you are all so eager to learn. Yet when I talk with your wives, they say you don't want to hear one suggestion. Is the difference that I'm so much more fascinating, delightful, and brilliant? Don't I wish! No, it's simply that you don't have to live with me. I can fill you with advice (and even admonitions) and you'll accept it, but when it comes from a wife or child, it seems to be an attack. When you live with the one who carries the shears, you tend to resist the cuts. From here on pray that the Lord will give you the ability to accept the pruning as His will to shape you into the gracious person He intends you to be. Listen to the suggestions. Maybe you do spend too much time away from home. Maybe you do have some sucker shoots that drain your energy and need to be pruned off. God is the Gardener, and He'll prune you until you become a winner.

Win the blue ribbon.

It takes so little to be above average

PART II

*It Takes So
Little to Think
Above Average*

CHAPTER EIGHT

Realize We Don't Think Much

*I*t doesn't take much to think above average because the average person doesn't think much. Henry James, the turn-of-the century psychologist, said that the average person uses only ten percent of his available brain-power. Do you see how little extra you would have to think to be above average? If you exerted only two percent beyond your norm, you would be on your way; if you doubled your thinking capacity, you would be close to brilliant!

It sounds so simple. Why aren't we all thinking our way to success?

The first reason is that we didn't know we weren't doing it. We thought we were thinking. When I first started teaching CLASS, I had no lesson on thinking. I assumed we all knew how to do that. Since we were a group of Christian leaders, certainly we must be thinkers. As the seminar grew, I began to get an amazing and consistent reaction: "I didn't know I could think this hard"; "I didn't realize my brain wasn't really working"; "My mind hasn't been turned on for 14 years."

As I became aware that individuals were learning to think in our seminar (and I wasn't even teaching the subject), I wondered what would happen if I began to teach it—and how I would approach it.

The average person has always been a little afraid of deep thinkers, mystics, or ivory-tower people. As Julius Caesar said, "Yond Cassius has a lean and hungry look; he thinks too much: such men are dangerous."[1]

We don't want to be peculiar; we want to be relevant. Surely, we are not like Cassius in thinking too much. When my son was in sixth grade, I found as I questioned him about his English homework that he didn't know a noun from a verb. Having been an English teacher, I was aghast that he had somehow missed "parts of speech." I went to his teacher at the Christian school he attended and asked her where Fred had been when she taught nouns. Her answer was, "We don't teach those things anymore. No one really needs to know them to get along in life." She was right in one way. Fred doesn't know them, and he is still alive.

If you don't know a noun and verb, you can't know a clause. If you don't know a clause, you don't know how to punctuate. If you can't place a comma or a period in the right spot, your sentences all run together. No wonder most high school graduates can't construct a complete paragraph and need their mothers to write their college application letters.

Several years after I realized that the simple basics of education were not being taught to my son, the National Commission on Excellence in Education came out with a scathing report on the present condition of our schools. "A tide of mediocrity has devastated public education. If an unfriendly foreign power had attempted to impose on America the mediocre educational performance that exists today, we might well have viewed it as an act of war."[2]

Carolyn Kane in an inspired article, "Thinking: A Neglected Art," writes:

> Intelligence is just as much a part of human nature as sociability. It would certainly be unnatural for a person to allow his mind to die of neglect. . . . If we are to survive as a free people, we will have to take some courses of action as soon as possible, because regardless of what some advertisers have led us to believe, this country does not run on oil. It runs on ideas.[3]

I remember my freshman year in high school when I had to take Latin. No one wanted to take Latin; we had to if we wanted to go to college. We complained and murmured, "Why do we have to take Latin? It's a dead language."

Miss McCormick's assignment to us was to write a conversation in Latin. We got together after school and decided this was asking us too much. Who could converse in a dead language? If none of us did the lesson, we wouldn't be in trouble. The next morning Miss McCormick asked, "How many of you decided this lesson was too hard for you?" We raised our hands. "Were there any of you who did it?" To our amazement, several hands went up. Miss McCormick called these spoilers up and read their scripts back and forth with them. Simple, sensible sentences. We could all understand them.

When the exercise was over, she kept these students up front and stated, "In every group there are always a limited few who are above average. The majority of you did the average thing. You decided the assignment was unfair and too difficult. You had no trouble finding friends whose goals were no higher than your own. These students before you also knew the lesson was close to impossible, but they decided to do it anyway. They pushed their minds beyond their past abilities, and they achieved results. Are you going to spend your lives being average and supporting yourselves with excuses, or are you going to be among those few who achieve the impossible?"

We were all humbled, disliking those few who had been praised, but we stopped looking for legitimate ways out of our Latin lessons. Within the month we were all conversing in simple Latin sentences.

Have I ever needed to speak Latin? No. Was that year wasted time because it wasn't practical? Oh no. I learned Latin roots, prefixes, and suffixes that doubled my English vocabulary and which have served me well ever since, but most of all I learned to stretch my mind beyond the possible to above average.

Today very few students have to take Latin or learn to diagram a sentence. We are keeping much of our education practical. As the Commission on Excellence stated in their report, our schools are offering "a cafeteria-style curriculum in which the appetizers and desserts can easily be mistaken for the main course."4

When Marita was a senior in high school, she took two units of work experience, which meant she got credit for waitressing in a coffee shop which we owned—plus she got tips. Not only did she earn money, but we also sent in her grade for the work experience. Naturally, she got A's! She also got an A in scuba diving. She was the only girl in her class and the life of the party. Her other class was called "Community Lab," where it was suggested she visit city hall and the county museum at any convenient time and write one report for the term. This was surely a cafeteria-style curriculum.

A few years ago the State of California came up with a unique thought: Why not make up a competency test for new teachers? To check its validity, they gave the test to current teachers. The newspaper headlines reflected the public's shock when they proclaimed that many of the present teachers couldn't pass the competency test in their own subject. When the standards are low enough, it takes almost nothing to be above average.

If we wish to raise the level of our thinking power, we first have to recognize that we don't really think much. We tend to do a lot and think a little. We feel that intellectual activity is akin to laziness; we don't see tangible results from meditation.

My mother, having struggled for survival through the Depression, never could understand work that wasn't "normal." My brother Ron is the top radio personality in Dallas, and he spends much of his time thinking up ways to keep his station number one. His office is a dimly lit room where he can lean back in a comfortable chair and "let the muses float free." After visiting him, my mother said, "I can't believe he even earns money sitting around thinking up those tomfool ideas! I wonder if he'll ever grow up and get a real job."

Thinking doesn't show, and its results later appear to be momentary flashes. Thinking takes time and determination.

Carolyn Kane says, "Even Einstein had to study and think for months before he could formulate his theory of relativity. Those of us who are less intelligent find it a struggle to conceive even a moderately good idea, let alone a brilliant one."[5]

Are we basically in agreement that we don't think a lot?
Then what should we do about it?

Today look back on your education and begin to fill in the blanks.

ADDITIONAL CHALLENGES FOR MEN:

Frequently, I talk with men who tell me they haven't read
a book in years. These are intelligent, successful men who are
doing what has to be done each day, but not putting any new
ideas into their minds. One man had entered network marketing in addition to his regular job, and he reported, "I had
no idea how much time I wasted each day until I started to
read. I hadn't picked up a book since I got out of high school,
but my sponsor kept suggesting books. I told him I had no
time to read, but he gave me your *Personality Plus* and insisted
I read it. I carried it around with me and worked it into odd
moments and couldn't believe I read it in two days. Now I
read two motivational books a week, and I can feel a difference in my ability to think. Tell men there's a lot to be learned
out there that we won't find on television."

Realize we don't think much.

It takes so little to be above average.

CHAPTER NINE

Decide to Improve Our Minds

*T*he Bible tell us, "As [a man] thinketh in his heart, so is he" (Proverbs 23:7). This verse explains why those of us who don't think much don't amount to much and demonstrates the power the mind has over the body. Abraham Lincoln said, "A man's about as happy as he sets out to be." The human mind is amazingly open to suggestions, and it will grasp onto whatever we feed it.

When we tell our minds we will fail, we often do. As our schools have dropped the basics from their curricula in order to teach practical skills and brotherly love, they have instead ironically produced bodies that can't think and people who don't even like each other. Brotherly love and busing in place of basics simply hasn't worked. The school report shows: "Each generation of Americans has outstripped its parents in education, in literacy and in economic attainment. For the first time in the history of our country, the educational skills of one generation will not surpass, will not equal, will not even approach, those of their parents."[1]

Response to this shocking evaluation has stirred a flood of protest, and the *Los Angeles Times* has been printing letters on "The Sorry State of U.S. Schooling." Karen Chrisney of Arcadia wrote, "I believe that more mind-stimulating lessons should take the place of the tedious 'busy work,' which is all writing and very little thinking. In fact, a greater number of students might actually do their homework if it were more appealing to them."[2]

As we have drifted away from the basics of thought-provoking education and have dropped discipline for free-thinking, no one is thinking at all. Don Bresnahan, producer of TV documentaries for KABC, Los Angeles, wrote in *Newsweek*, "People don't want to think seriously or for very long." He tells how he formerly produced "serious issue-oriented half-hour and hour-long documentaries." But the Nielson ratings showed that the public didn't want anything so deep. "They tell us that you viewers have an attention span of no more than a minute to a minute and a half. That's why we race from story to story, giving you peaks and valleys . . . If we don't tell our stories quickly and necessarily briefly, we might lose you to some more frivolous activity like reading a book or brushing your teeth."[3] Now Mr. Bresnahan produces "minidocs": quick, easily digested chunks spread out over five nights.

But the tide appears to be turning. I was amazed to find a drawing of a brain on the cover of *U.S. News and World Report* (January 24, 1983). Since cover subjects indicate areas of interest among the general public, I was encouraged with their article dividing the brain into sections which control our emotions and telling us of new information on the power of the brain. Two weeks later (February 7, 1983), *Newsweek* had a cartoon head on the cover labeled "The

Human Computer—How the Brain Works." In April, *Reader's Digest* showed silhouetted heads full of numbers with their lead article, "Seven Steps to Better Thinking." That same month *The Toastmaster* applauded "Whole Mind Power."

There seems to be an interest in the brain. *Newsweek* says:

> The mind has always been dumbfounded by the brain. That three-pound glob of matter hardly seems up to the task of writing "Paradise Lost," composing "Eroica" or discovering relativity. Yet for 2,400 years, ever since Hippocrates located the seat of the intellect inside the skull, the mind has been forced to admit that its greatest achievements, its loftiest thoughts, its deepest emotions all arise from something with the consistency of Jell-O and the color of day-old slush.[4]

Interest in the brain has increased over the last ten years, especially in the area of control over the thinking process and physical ailments. *Time* (July 17, 1995) showed a brain on the cover with the title "In Search of the Mind." Scientists peer into the brain looking for that evanescent thing called "consciousness." The article said:

> In response to this enormous opportunity— not just to clarify the mysteries of consciousness but also to understand and treat such devastating mind malfunctions as Alzheimer's disease, depression, drug addiction . . . research projects have multiplied dramatically. . . . In short, the brain is a hot topic.[5]

What the brain can actually do may always be a mystery:

> Neuroscientists may have pulled memory and
> emotion under their reductionist umbrella, argue
> the skeptics, but surely will and consciousness will
> escape them. In fact, the brain's very complexity
> will postpone the day when it is finally explained
> by common forces.[6]

They've figured out many complexities of the brain, but they can't master the human will. God gave us our own free will, and no outside force can quickly change or even understand it. I'm reminded of the story of the little boy whose mother made him sit in the corner. He looked up and said, "I may be sitting on the outside, but I'm standing up inside."

Our will is within our own control. Are you going to determine today to push it that extra mile toward discovery and creativity? Let's assume you are a mature person who has recognized you don't do a lot of deep thinking and who has decided to improve your mind. What can you do about it? Ted Turner, chairman of Turner Broadcasting System and owner of the Atlanta Braves and Hawks, said in an interview, "I believe the brain is a muscle, and like any other muscle, the more you use it the stronger it gets. You almost have to teach yourself to think more."[7]

Whether you think of your brain as Jell-O, day-old slush, or a muscle, you can agree that it's an amazing apparatus and has limitless possibilities. You don't have to understand it to appreciate it.

One day in the middle of a speaking engagement I made the statement that God does not waste any of our experiences in life. At that same instant it came to me, "What about those years you spent playing bridge? What good have they done you as a Christian speaker?" While I was still speaking, some remote parts of my mind were having this discussion, and I suddenly realized I was able to talk and think on different tracks at the same time. Instantly, I answered my original question: Years of playing bridge had taught me to think on four tracks: clubs, diamonds, hearts, and spades! God had not wasted my ability to quickly file those 52 cards in columns in my brain. The ability was still intact; He had just changed the labels on the tracks.

On the way home that day, I asked myself what my present tracks were labeled. I now realized I was thinking of more than one thing at a time, and this was surely an asset to my speaking, but what were my tracks doing? I had already been conducting CLASS, and I was constantly breaking the skills I had into teachable units so that I could communicate them to others. As I analyzed my thinking, I could see my first speaking track was full of material—subject matter from my life experiences, memories of my childhood, collections of prose and poetry I had studied, Bible verses I had learned.

My second track was my ability to outline my material ahead of time, to organize my thoughts, to shorten or change my order while speaking. As I thought of these two tracks, I realized they were essential for effective elocution. Without something to say, there would be no reason to speak. Without any organization, there would be no way to remember the message.

Added to these two came my response track, the one that is open to the Readings of the Holy Spirit, hearing His voice of suggestions, and also responsive to the needs and attitudes of people. Without a firm hold on one's material and a simple outline to hold it all together, there would be no opening for a response track.

When all three of these are working concurrently, there is a desire to communicate the inner feelings of one's conscience, one's emotions, one's heart to the listener. This genuine sharing of one's own life is what makes hearers remember you as a person they can relate to and learn from. In order to communicate effectively, whether on the platform or in conversation, we need to have all four tracks working simultaneously. We need to have something to say, the Material track. We need to give the material in an organized manner so that people will remember it, the Organization track. We then need to be open to the leadings of the Lord and the desires of our audience—one or more—so we are flexible with our material and structure, the Response track. And most important in reaching the hearts of people, we need genuine emotion, concern, and vulnerability. The people have to see we care, the Emotion track.

There's an expression that's popular today: "People don't care how much you know until they know how much you care."

Do you have all four tracks running concurrently? If you don't, you can. The equipment is all there!

As these simple concepts of how my brain worked appeared to me, I realized the term "one-track mind" came from people who could only hold one set of ideas together at a time. Have you met people with one-track minds? What a waste when we have limitless tracks available and waiting to be used.

As I began to teach participants in the seminars to think

on four tracks, we developed an acrostic to help us remember how to communicate more effectively:

Material
Organization
Response
Emotion

As Christians we need to be able to think MORE than we've done in the past. You may not have checked your mind recently to find out what its potentials are, but start stretching and training a four-track mind. *Time* said of defeated English labor leader Michael Foot: "He displayed an impressive ability to talk for hours without a text, but his train of thought was occasionally derailed."[8]

Today begin a dinner-table discussion about one of today's headlines.

ADDITIONAL CHALLENGES FOR MEN:

It is amazing how often a man comes up to me and says, "I don't usually like women speakers, but you're different. You think like a man!" This is always meant as a compliment (inferring that women either don't think at all or do so on such a low level as to be of no substance or interest to men).

Researchers do tell us that men have greater powers of reasoning and structure than women do, while women are better at intuition and sensitivity. Neither is right or wrong, only different.

But, dear men, don't rest on your laurels of brilliance! Instead, start stretching your minds ever further. Before you make a presentation at the office or church or even to your

family, ask yourself if you really have anything to say
(Material), if you have thought it out in such a way that it
makes clear sense and is memorable (Organization), if you
have enough flexibility to be open-minded (Response), and
if you are speaking from your heart in a kind way to the
hearts of the hearers (Emotion).

If I can think like a man, surely you can, too.

Decide to improve your mind.

It does take something to be above average.

CHAPTER TEN

Set Aside a Think Spot

*B*efore we can get down to actually improving our minds, we should set aside some spot where we can think quietly and without interruption. Because we don't take the time and effort to remove ourselves from the confusion of life, we have difficulty doing much creative thinking. The Lord Jesus taught us the value of withdrawing to a quiet place to pray and to think. Do you have such a spot? Do you already have a place for your daily quiet time? If not, this might be the start of something new.

Some people have a desk, a corner table, an easy chair. One woman I know drives to a camellia garden, one walks by the shore, one sits in her car overlooking the city. My favorite spot is in my bathroom. I have a tub with a carpeted step up to it, and I lay my Bible there and sit on the floor. A ledge behind the tub holds pots of African violets, and the window opens into a plant-filled atrium. This spot is beautiful to look at and peaceful to my soul. It is here that I've prayed through some difficult times in my life. It is a special place where I can be still and know that He is Almighty God.

Airplanes are "think spots" for me also. When I finish a three-day CLASS and sink into a seat on the plane, I am alone, able to sort out the seminar, able to jot down creative ideas and improvements before I forget them.

Robert Anderson, chairman of Atlantic-Richfield, once said, "Flying has provided a major part of the time that I can devote to thinking. It is an isolated environment; there are no telephones, and there is no way anyone can intrude on your thoughts."[1]

Anne Ortlund, in her book *Disciplines of the Beautiful Woman*, emphasizes the need for a daily quiet time, and she frequently goes to a restaurant to spend some reflective moments. Once a month she and her husband, Ray, go away for a special day of thinking.

Many of you may want to combine your daily devotions with your thinking time. God asks that we put Him first, give Him our first ten percent. As we pray and read God's Word, we can open our minds to His direction and let His thoughts stimulate ours. "Let this mind be in you, which was also in Christ Jesus."[2]

As we begin to realize how little time we spend in solitary meditation, is it any wonder our brain is only functioning at one-tenth of its potential? George Ball, Corporate Executive Officer of Prudential-Bache Securities, says:

I set aside time to think twice a day. First, early in the morning when I am still at home and before my family is up, I set 10-15 minutes for undisciplined, freewheeling thought—whether it's about the state of the universe or the state of my fountain pen. When I am headed home from

work, I try to have 15 minutes or so for idea-gath-
ering. At the end of the day one is less fresh and
therefore less creative. But I try to put together
the ideas I want to concentrate subliminally on
overnight and think about the next morning.[3]

If you wish to speed up your thinking process, start by
finding a "think spot" and setting aside time to use it. Once
you find how much fun it is to expand your creative ability,
you will see "think spots" everywhere: in your car, in line at
the supermarket, in the dentist's waiting room, in church.
Make use of them; think constantly.

*Today find a quiet spot, relax, and let the Lord fill your mind
with creative thoughts.*

ADDITIONAL CHALLENGES FOR MEN:

Is there anywhere in your home where you can sit and
think? Does your family understand that you need some time
alone where you can plan, pray, and prepare for the future?
Where you can get on a level above report cards and dripping
faucets? If you could find such a place, would you use it or
would you still collapse in front of the television and watch
whatever game happens to be in season? Fred and I have
always had a pair of comfortable chairs in our bedroom, and
we trained our children to stay out of our room when the door
was shut. In an emergency, they could knock but never barge
in. We made our mutual think spot in the bedroom. Now that
we are alone, we still spend quiet time, either together or separately, in those chairs in the bedroom or on the bed.

Fred sets his alarm 15 minutes early so we have time to
sit up, have a cup of coffee, and think creatively about the

day ahead of us. Fred is the one who sets the timer on the coffeepot the night before and then serves coffee to me in the morning. When we're in hotels, he goes down to the lobby, gets the coffee, and brings it back to the room. I appreciate his part in making our quiet time together each morning so special.

Men, be the one to create a special time and place for creative thinking and intimate conversation. Your wife will be delighted.

Set aside a think spot and then use it!

It takes so little to be above average.

CHAPTER ELEVEN

Start With the Past

*P*icture your brain as a file cabinet. Since statistics show we are using only one-tenth of our available mental space, let's be specific. Let's picture our brain as a large file cabinet with ten drawers. The bottom one is jammed with assorted information in no particular order. The facts aren't even in manila folders. Some thoughts are so old that the edges have turned yellow, and some new ideas are sitting outside the drawer in a pile waiting to be sorted. Above this one eclectic drawer are nine empty ones. Once in a while after a brilliant lecture, you put a piece of the program in an empty drawer, intending to go back and add to the subject later. But you've been so busy with the basics of life that you only have one drawer in operation—that bottom one labeled "Average."

There's so much brain space available, yet we've crowded everything into one drawer. Where do we begin? We dedicate our thinking time to an introspective view of the past. Let's put our former life experiences into folders and label them for quick access when needed. We're told our brain contains everything we've ever seen or heard, but some of our memory is so remote we can't put our hands on the facts. If we wish to stir up our reservoir of knowledge, that wealth of information we have stored away, we must reminisce, pull the color out of the confusion, and start using some of the empty drawers.

In CLASS we have a lesson on "How You Filled Your Reservoir in the Past," where we list some items that will jog your memory. As you read the following ideas, jot down the incidents that come to your mind. If you were to read this list every day, you would still come up with new thoughts. Each time I teach this lesson, I remember new, colorful examples from the past to add to my reservoir.

At first you may see no use in rehashing old events, but as you begin to reach for the past, your brain will throw itself in high gear and begin working in a new way. You'll be amazed at what you remember when you try. If you do any kind of speaking, such as teaching a Bible study or presenting a business plan, you will be excited over the fascinating examples you can find from your own life. If you do any writing, this mental exercise will stir your creative juices. Why not take a notebook and title each page with one of the following headings? As you begin to fill in the blank pages, you will increase your reservoir and will actually compile a biographical sketch of your life. These 12 pages from the past will inspire you to journalize the present to use in the future.

As I list the topics, let your mind wander. Pause for a few moments. Write down what appears. Don't rush. Relax.

Hometown Atmosphere

Where did you grow up? What kind of a town was it? What was your house like? How did it differ from the homes of your friends? Were there any special places to play or hide? What positive memory do you have of your environment?

I lived in three rooms behind my father's store in Haverhill, Massachusetts, a shoe-factory town, once chosen by a Rand McNally survey as the least-desirable city in which to live in the entire United States. As children we ate our meals in front of the customers, and to go from one bedroom where all five of us slept in layers to the bathroom, we had to pass the cash register. All my friends had regular houses, and in my teen years I was embarrassed to live in a store. Behind us were two auto-repair shops, and when my brothers went out to play with cars, they really played with cars. In spite of the disadvantages, we all learned how to get along with people since we lived with our customers from 6:30 in the morning until 11 o'clock at night, seven days a week. What do you remember about your hometown?

Nationality Blends

What kind of yarns are you woven from? Are you all one stock, or are you a mixed breed? Does your background have any influence over your personality or current lifestyle? What nationality blends do your children have?

My father was born in England. He taught me poems, stories, and tongue twisters from the time I was very young and constantly stretched my imagination. His emphasis on language and vocabulary has had a definite impact on my life and that of my two brothers. My mother is Scottish-Canadian, and as a child wore kilts and marched in a bagpipe band beside her father. Since my husband is German, my children are one-quarter English, one-quarter Scotch, and one-half German. What is your blend?

Childhood Relationships

What do you remember about your feelings about your brothers and sisters? Was there a special friend who influenced your life? How did you relate to your parents?

I always wanted a sister, and little Jim was so beautiful that I would dress him up in my old clothes and pretend he was a girl. When my brother Ron was born, I was so upset that he was a boy that I took him to the top of our street in his carriage and then let it wheel freely into the traffic. Gratefully, the carriage hit a tree and stopped safely. The incident so frightened me that I became slavishly devoted to my baby brother.

My girlfriend Peggy was everything I wanted to be. She had a turned-up nose, and long, thick blond hair. She was popular at school and lived in a real house. When we went window-shopping, I would wait until she said what was pretty and then agree with her. I didn't want to voice an opinion that might differ from Peggy's.

Are you beginning to have an idea of how to review and record your past? Do you see how easy it is to stimulate your brain into resourceful thinking? Now you fill in the remaining topics without my giving you examples.

Education and Other Training

How far back can you remember in your schooling? Who's the first teacher you can recall? Can you remember anything she taught you? What kind of a grammar school did you go to? What was your high school like? Was there any special teacher who influenced your life? Did you take any outside training? Did you win any contests, letters, or awards?

Talents and Hobbies

What kind of talent did you have as a child? Did you take any lessons? How did your parents compare your talent with theirs? With your brothers and sisters? Did your early talent have any bearing on your career? What hobbies have you had in life? How have they been productive in the past? Is there any talent you really wish you'd had?

Odd Jobs and Careers

What was your first job? What kind of a boss did you have? What did you learn from it? What was your most unusual job? Which job helped you shape your career choice? What career changes have you had as an adult?

Courtship and Marriage

Where did you and your mate meet and under what circumstances? What differences did you have in background, religion, personality? How did you first know your relationship was serious? Who proposed, and where were you at the time? How long was your engagement, and what can you remember of this romantic time in your life? Where was the wedding held? What was the church or building like? What colors were the bridal party's dresses? What flowers were carried? Where did you go on your honeymoon? What lessons did you learn in early marriage? What problems have you worked to overcome? What has been the most important bond between you and your partner?

Organizations and Leadership

List in sequence all the different groups you've been a part of until now. Is there any consistency? Add next to each title any office you held in the group. Is there any similarity? Which organization did you most enjoy and why? Which did you contribute the most to, and was this work appreciated? What leadership skills do you feel you have?

Churches Attended

List the different churches or denominations you have attended. What pastor can you remember best? What Sunday school teacher influenced your life and how? What church activities were you involved in, such as choir, Sunday school teaching, missionary society? In retrospect, what quality of religious training did you receive? What lasting values have you retained from your church attendance? Have you changed churches? Why?

Christian Commitment

When did you first commit your life to Jesus Christ? What made you realize you needed a Savior? What person was influential in your decision? What changes has your commitment made on your life? How have you been sharing your faith with others? What Bible studies have you attended? Have you taught any?

Family Circumstances

How old were you when your first child was born? Where were you living at the time? What circumstances changed in your marriage with the addition of children? What is special about each one of your children? Write a few sentences on each one. How has your life influenced their spiritual growth? Behavior? Education? Career choice?

Traumas, Illnesses, and Victories

What is the most traumatic event of your life? In retrospect, what caused the situation? What was the most difficult part of the problem? What did you learn from it? List the major illnesses you've had. Which ones have had lasting effects on you? Have you had any difficult hospital experiences? What is your overall attitude on illness and poor health? In looking back over your life circumstances, what have been your greatest victories? How could you share these experiences to give hope to others?

Once you have thoughtfully answered these questions in sequence, you will have enough recycled material to fill a whole drawer in your mental file cabinet. You will have these past thoughts brought up-to-date, and they will be in order. You could turn this time of questioning yourself into a family activity. You could use one of these topics each night at dinner or each Sunday afternoon. You could include guests since everyone loves to tell stories of their youth, and you will learn things about your family and friends that you didn't know before.

My son-in-law, Randy, sat down with my 85-year-old mother the year before she died and asked her to reminisce about the old days. He had previously set up the video camera without her knowledge, and she freely recalled her youth, marriage, attitudes about children, and personal feelings. What a blessing it is to all of us to have her own words recorded for future generations.

We have received such excellent responses from CLASS members who have written us later to let us know what a meaningful experience it has been to record the events and feelings of the past. One lady typed hers up, made copies, put them into folders, and gave one to each child for Christmas.

Take time to review your life and write it down. As you find a "think spot" and let your mind wander, ideas and life stories will come which you can add to your reservoir. Save these pages to insert into your journal (we'll discuss journalizing in chapter 13).

If you want to increase your mental ability, start with the past.

Don't be too busy with the present to reflect on the lessons of the past.

You are the world's greatest expert on you!

Today start your record of past experiences. Take out some old photographs, put names and dates on the back where you can, and use them to illustrate your life story.

ADDITIONAL CHALLENGES FOR MEN:

Wives complain to me that the only time their husbands sit down is to watch television and make phone calls. "He just won't sit and talk to me or even to the children." If this is a valid complaint in your house, this chapter will give you a great place to start in creative conversation with your family. Discuss where you lived as a child and how you felt about it. Share about relationships with your siblings, both positive and negative. Tell about humorous jobs you had when you were young. Let your family see that you're a real person.

They view enough actors on television each day. Let them enjoy Dad as a father who cares and shares, not just as a disciplinarian or wage-earner.

If you wish to increase the intimacy in your marriage, read our book *Freeing Your Mind From Memories That Bind*, and answer the questions and discuss them openly. You will learn things about each other you never knew before.

Start with your past.

It takes so little to be above average.

CHAPTER TWELVE

Be Alert to
the Present

So many people go through life with blinders on and heads down, seeing none of the beauty or the events around them. With so little effort we can be alert and find excitement everywhere. I glean fascinating examples for my speaking every day in many ways. You, too, can become a much better conversationalist when you are alert to life.

One of my best sources of colorful material is the beauty shop. When I arrive, the ladies ask where I've been and where I'm going, and soon all the customers are listening. To get new information, I have only to throw out a topic and see what the reaction is. Everyone has something to say, yet so few people have anyone who will listen.

One December I told them I was leaving for Oklahoma City to do a TV show on Christmas depression. Immediately, a college girl told me so many students were depressed that the school had hired a psychologist to lecture on the subject. One lady volunteered that she became depressed each year because there was always a fight over which family to spend the day with, and eventually everyone ended up mad during Christmas dinner. An elderly lady had tears in her eyes as she lamented she couldn't cook a big dinner anymore, and she had to depend on others. One girl had just moved to our area and was depressed because she couldn't afford to go home for Christmas. A widow confessed how she dreaded all holidays, and a young girl related how her brother had committed suicide on Christmas Eve.

I took notes as these women shared the burdens and depressions of their hearts, trying to console each other. Upon arriving for the TV show, I was preceded by an intellectual professor of psychiatry who spoke analytically of the problem of Christmas depression, as if it were past tense. He was deep, dull, and remote. When I was asked to make what he had said relevant, I was able to say, "People are depressed right now. Let me give you some current examples of ladies I've spoken with this week." How much more impact we can have on others when we know what's going on *this* week.

The Toastmaster had a fascinating article, "Thank God It's Monday." It stated:

> Perhaps you say, "My brain doesn't start functioning in the morning until after my third cup of coffee." That's too late. Force your mind to become productive as you arise. Your thoughts are important. They don't just evaporate like the morning mist. They are with you all day long. Be alert. Focus your mind on current issues and situations.[1]

Be alert to people of interest in rest rooms, at the check-out counter, in airports. Some need your smile, some your hand on a shoulder, some your words of wisdom.

As the staff and I travel together, I constantly challenge them to keep thinking, to notice people and situations around them. One day Patsy Clairmont met us in San Francisco and could hardly wait to tell us of her adventure on the plane. She was already seated when a couple entered and stopped at her row. They looked at the seat behind Patsy, demanding the lady sitting there to get out since that was their seat assignment. The lady answered, "No speak English." They yelled at her, and still the same answer. The man called for the flight attendant and demanded the lady's removal. She shrugged again, unable to understand why everyone was upset with her. Patsy told us that normally she would have ignored the problem, but because of our emphasis on being alert to life, she stood up and volunteered to give the couple her seat, which had an empty one next to it. The attendant thanked her, and the couple sat down.

Noticing the lady's seat belt was not fastened, Patsy stretched it out to its very fullest (the woman was rather large) and just barely got it shut. Patsy smiled at the lady and patted her on the hand. A few minutes later the lady reached over, took Patsy's hand in hers, and pressed something into her palm. As Patsy looked she saw a gold chain bracelet and asked, "What's this for?" The lady, with a tear in her eye, stammered, "You first American be nice to me." Patsy was touched in telling the incident. She showed us the bracelet and shared the lady's last words to her: "You wear. You remember me?"

That week I urged Patsy to relate this tale to show how much of life's flavor we miss when we are not alert to what's going on around us. As you tune in more closely with your surroundings, you will feel your mind moving and your material track expanding.

Another obvious way to fill up the emptiness in our minds is to read everything, everywhere, at all times. If you're in the doctor's office and his magazines are 12 years old, rejoice. You can see firsthand how people were thinking then and compare it with the present for better or for worse.

Read the paper each day. I try to at least glance through the paper before I go out each day. Even if I am teaching a seminar at 9:00 A.M., I see what happened overnight before going. I turn on one of the morning news shows while dressing and have an overview of the world before I leave to speak. It takes so little time to be above average. I find people amazed that I, the speaker, have read the paper when they, the audience, are still buttoning their blouses.

As an experiment, I took ten *Time* magazine covers with pictures of people sufficiently prominent and current to be known around the world. I held them up in front of the audience and had the people write down the name of each person. Upon correcting the papers, we found that the average member of these above-average groups had three out of ten right.

If we leaders don't know what's going on in the world, who does?

Bruce Bawer, English teacher at the State University of New York at Stony Brook, wrote in an article entitled "Ignorance (Not Stupidity) Is Rampant on College Campuses":

> College students today are amazingly lacking in important knowledge, and it's no laughing matter. . . . If I were dealing with simpletons, none of this would bother me profoundly. But my students are not simple-minded. Most get good marks in their major subjects, and many intend careers in medicine, engineering, law. Far from

being "slow," they are intelligent, and on their way to becoming the "leaders of tomorrow." But they do not have the knowledge that a college student, let alone a leader, ought to have. . . .

It is up to the individual parent to influence these tastes and interests as positively as possible. For example, buy the kid a few books instead of a video game. Put a globe in his room and look at it with him every now and then. Take him to a symphony concert so that he will be able to appreciate Mozart as well as Meatloaf when he grows up (and recognize the name). Walk him through the local museum on a Saturday after-noon. Keep an atlas, a dictionary, a history book, and a set of encyclopedias around the house, and make conspicuous use of them. Ration the TV. A little imagination on the part of a parent can go a long way toward helping a child learn.

. . . It is not the most systematic method of education, but it is, at present, the only way to keep the most advanced civilization on earth from producing the most inexcusably ignorant generation of college graduates in its history. [2]

Long before Professor Bawer was teaching, my father had the same idea. He not only read the paper each day, but he also gave us children capsulized versions of the day's news before we went to school. As I look back on it, I'm sure much of our success was due to his keeping our minds alert to life. During political campaigns he taught us the issues and made us care who won.

I've followed his pattern in raising my children to be

alert to the present. This policy takes dedication on our part and a willingness to read, study, and digest so that we can disseminate our knowledge attractively enough for our children to listen.

Today read at least one newspaper and find one item worthy of sharing with your family.

ADDITIONAL CHALLENGES FOR MEN:

In many families the mother is too busy to keep up with the times, and this responsibility falls upon the father. Pick this opportunity up and share with the family not only what you did all day, but also what has happened in the world since you left this morning. Have them listen to the news with you, turn on the State of the Union message, tune in to Rush Limbaugh. You may or may not agree with him, but he will keep you up-to-date on today's hot topics, and you'll laugh while learning.

Because my father got me interested in politics at an early age, I have always followed the personalities of the different candidates and kept my children apprised of the differences. If you have even a slight interest in political personalities, you will enjoy my book *Put Power in Your Personality*. There is enough information in there to keep you conversing brightly for months.

With ignorance being rampant in the world today, be alert to the present.

It takes so little to be above average.

CHAPTER THIRTEEN

Journalize for the Future

*W*e have seen the value of recording the past and being alert to the present. Now let's learn how to journalize for the future. As we begin to write down today's thoughts, we record patterns which will help us to understand ourselves in the future.

What Is Journalizing?

In *The Toastmaster* it says, "Unlike a diary a journal is not an hour-by-hour listing of what happens each day, but a recording of thoughts and feelings. It's an unstructured writing out of the events of your life . . . *as you see them.* It gives you a true perspective of the world and your role in it. A journal, done properly, is an intensely personal experience."[1]

Because journalizing is an intensely personal experience where we openly lay down our inner lives, we need to write in private and keep our thoughts locked up. If we expect others to read our words, we will not be honest. Journalizing is a pouring out of our heart on paper.

How Do I Start?

Get yourself a notebook, or use your computer. Sit down and write whatever thoughts go through your head.

When you're confident no one is going to read your thoughts, it's amazing how fast they come and how deeply you dig. New York psychologist Ira Progoff records his "intensive journal" in a loose-leaf notebook with 21 colored dividers labeling different topics of his life. The form is not as important as the feelings. Journalizing becomes therapy for the writer, a time when you don't have to worry about what other people think of your ideas. Don't allow grammar, spelling, and punctuation to slow down your thoughts—just pour them out.

What Do I Say?

Some people write as if the words were a letter to themselves, some as if they were explaining their problems to a counselor, and some as if they were praying to God. As you focus your direction, start writing what comes to your mind. You may think you'll have nothing to say, but our experience tells us that as a woman sits down to be honest with herself, she often writes for hours, and when men decide to journalize, they write things down that they won't ever talk about. Jerry Labhart of Fort Worth wrote Francine Jackson about his first journalizing: "Your instruction of pouring out my feelings to God on paper is better than any tranquilizer on the market."

Jerry Mason, in "A Different Way to Pray," began journalizing to help in his prayer life. He got a notebook, sat down, and wrote six pages of "pent-up prayers":

> I write informally, not to impress but to communicate, conveying my heart in a way that works for me, using phrases such as these:
>
> —Dear God,
> —Tonight I feel . . .
> —I want to thank You for . . .
> —In Your Word You've told me to . .
> —I'm not sure I understand . . .
> —Father, help me to . . .
> —Today I . . .
> —I wonder . . .
> and much more.[2]

What Good Does Journalizing Do Me?

Your writing becomes a personal record of your inner life. As you look back over your thoughts, you will remember how you felt and see patterns of behavior which may need to be changed.

Tristine Rainer, author of *The New Diary*, says, "The diary is a never-ending process of search and discovery. It changes as you change; and by acting as a mirror to the self it encourages personal transformation."[3]

James Cummings, who has kept a diary since he was 13 years old, writes, "I feel that if you live an interesting life and are aware of it—if you go through each day and then record that day, it becomes a reciprocal process. You're living well to record well, and it goes on and on."

My friend Roseanne wrote me:

> I began my journal the Friday that Francine challenged us to do so. Writing in it has become the highlight of my day (I've written over two hundred pages since CLASS). Some days the words pour from my pen. Others, I have to force myself to write about things which are difficult. In writing about the hard things, I have found answers. I have not only learned to express myself on paper, but I can now verbally express myself to my husband without fear of rejection. I think he must have learned more about who I really am in the last three months than he did in our previous nineteen years of marriage.
>
> My journal has proved on numerous occasions to be a source of encouragement to me. At times when I began to go into depression, I picked up my journal and read how God had met my need in a similar situation.

One of the unexpected results of journalizing is that the writer learns how to communicate feelings on paper, and then is able to communicate feelings in person.

Roseanne sent us a section of her journal done in her "think spot"—a park an hour's drive from her home.

> Lord, suddenly I see my life, not as a mess, but as the background of a child's puzzle—the kind with the outlines of the pieces drawn on it. I see not hundreds of small pieces, but ten (I don't know why that number, Lord) neatly laid out around the edges. I feel an air of expectancy as if

suddenly You are going to pick up each piece and lay them neatly into place. I shed a lot of tears today, Lord, not tears of sadness, or depression, or feeling sorry for myself, but rather tears which just poured from me because of my sense of the overwhelming things You are doing in my life.

As you can see from Roseanne's writing, when she puts her thoughts on paper they become a beautiful collection of gems which, if strung together, could someday become a book. What we don't write down today, we may not remember tomorrow.

Is Journalizing Scriptural?

David was a master journalizer, and his psalms are ours today because he took the time to write down his feelings. He talked to God in a personal way, and his thoughts then are so like ours today. Look at Psalm 55, for one example. David is afraid for his life and he cries out to God:

> Give ear to my prayer, O God, and hide not thyself from my supplication. Attend unto me, and hear me: I mourn in my complaint, and make a noise; because of the voice of the enemy, because of the oppression of the wicked: for they cast iniquity upon me, and in wrath they hate me (verses 1-3).

Have you ever felt like David? Do you ever cry out to the Lord? "Listen, God! Listen. Don't hide from me. Where are You when I need You? Can't You hear me crying and complaining? People are talking about me and turning against me. They framed me, and now everyone thinks it's my fault, and they all hate me."

> My heart is sore pained within me: and the terrors of death are fallen upon me. Fearfulness and trembling are come upon me, and horror hath overwhelmed me (verses 4,5).

"My stomach's in knots, I think I'm dying. I'm scared to death, my hands are shaking, and I feel like the victim in a horror movie."

> I said, Oh, that I had wings like a dove! for then would I fly away, and be at rest. Lo, then would I wander far off, and remain in the wilderness (verses 6,7).

"Oh God, get me out of here. Let me fly away and have a moment of peace. If only I could get out of these circumstances, I could be happy. Oh God, even the desert looks good to me now!"

Don't David's words sound familiar? Don't the words of the past have meaning for the present to help us in the future? If David can do it, so can you.

Nancy Williams came to our Dallas CLASS, a victim of agoraphobia—the paralyzing fear of being in open spaces. For 20 years she had kept this fear to herself and had only gone out of the house when her husband was with her. She amazed herself when she stood up in the small group and confessed this fear to the other ladies. This outpouring of her heart brought instant support from the others and began

Nancy's healing. I suggested she start writing a journal of her feelings as she worked her way out of her phobia. I didn't hear from her, so one day as I was in the Dallas airport I gave her a call to ask how she was doing. She sounded like a different person as she explained, "When you told me to write it all down, I didn't think I could do it, but I sat down with the paper and wrote sentences for six hours. I think I'm writing a book!"

It's amazing what can happen when we sit down with pen in hand and start to write.

Ruth Nichols of Fort Worth went home from CLASS and sat down to journalize. She took separate pieces of paper and put a heading on each one:

- Things I must do
- Things I need to do
- Things I would like to do
- Things I could do
- Things I enjoy doing
- Things I would be doing if I had the talent, nerve, ability, and/or confidence (my fantasy)
- Things I don't like about myself
- Things I can do to improve myself so I can then be able to help others
- Things I have done that I am proud of
- Things I have done to make money or as a career
- Things I have done or interests I have had over the last three months

After writing the headings, she went back to fill in what must be done or what she thought about each topic. By the last page, she had 36 different items listed.

The definition of *think* is to "devise a plan, form a mental picture of." By journalizing, you devise a plan. You commit your feelings to paper each day. As you review the journal, you form a mental picture of what your inner life was like at that moment.

So to journalize is to think, planning today to make mental pictures for the future.

Today begin to record those precious moments with the Lord.

ADDITIONAL CHALLENGES FOR MEN:

In most cases, men don't like to think about, talk about, and (especially) write about their feelings. They pride themselves on stuffing it all in and not letting emotions get them down. Then why would I suggest that you men start writing out your feelings and innermost thoughts? First, you are all above average or you wouldn't be reading this book. Second, if you went to a therapist for help, he would recommend that you journalize to get in touch with your feelings. (You can do this without paying the price of even one appointment.) Third, I've seen the tremendous change in my husband's life since he started writing out his prayers each day. He literally journalizes to the Lord. If he's unhappy with me—heaven forbid!—he tells the Lord about it instead of dropping his disappointments on me. He asks the Lord questions and writes the answers he receives in red ink. In the five years he's been writing, he has uncovered and worked through childhood trauma, business failures, and unforgiveness toward those who have hurt him. Writing his prayers has been not only therapeutic but also life-changing. We can now discuss feelings without getting angry. We both see where his feelings of rejection come from and can understand his reactions to perceived hurts.

Men, I can't emphasize enough how exciting it is for a woman to have a husband who is in touch with the Lord and with his feelings. Sit down somewhere *today* with a pad of paper or a computer and start to pour out your heart to the Lord.

Journalize for the future.

It takes so little today to be above average tomorrow.

CHAPTER FOURTEEN

Outline Life

*P*aul tells us in the Bible that we are to do all things decently and in order, and this guideline applies to our creative thinking. If our thoughts are to amount to anything, we must train them to move along in some semblance of order. Even creative thinking must have some form or sense of pattern, and we can change sloppy habits when we see value in a new mind-set.

So far we've been looking at the material we gather in our thinking, and we've filled our mental file drawers with our reservoir from the past, with alertness to life in the present, and with journalizing pages that will help us communicate better in the future. Now, how do we put our thoughts in order? To achieve our goal of thinking above average, we must begin to think in outline form. Many people have much material adrift in their heads but don't know how to organize it instantly to make the knowledge useful. A wise teacher makes learning a "joy."[1] Confusion is not an appealing condition, but orderly words are attractive; they make learning easy.

Whether you are ever going to speak, lead, or teach, or whether you just want to improve your communication with family and friends, you will profit by learning to think in outline form.

For many of you the mere mention of outlining reminds you of a high school or college composition class where outlining was overwhelming. Some serious teacher, intent upon stamping outlines indelibly in each little head, wrote ominous symbols on the blackboard: Roman numeral I, capital A, regular 1, little a, and so on. You knew you would never have any need for these indented lines, so you shut your mind to this lesson. But think again. Now that you're learning to use more than one mental track at a time, you will learn to outline and love it. God has already outlined life for us. In fact, God Himself is a three-point outline: Father, Son, Holy Spirit. He gave order to the universe when He created the earth in seven days, and He outlined our year in four seasons: spring, summer, autumn, winter; our calendar into 12 months; and our day into 24 hours. He arranged our lives into past, present, and future. He made each straight line to have a left, center, and right; positions to be up, down, or sideways; events to be good, bad, or indifferent.

These are all outlines, and all ones that we have previously memorized. Without any new instruction, we already know nine outlines without using one Roman numeral. God created order, and yet so many of our minds are floating in limbo with thoughts—even inspired thoughts—unattached to any form of organization. Is it not logical that if our minds are fuzzy, our daily lives can't be much better? If we wish to be above average, we must train our minds to do what they were originally made for: to think in logical order, to outline life!

Where do we start? Let's use one of the most valuable, simple outlines, sometimes called the "Five Journalistic W's": who, what, where, when, and why. Write them on a card and tape it near your phone until you have them memorized. Let's say you call a friend and get an answering machine. The average person either hangs up quickly or mumbles a few incoherent words, sometimes even forgetting to say who he is. As you train yourself to put life in order, you will use this simple outline:

Who: This is Joan Collins.
What: Our church is having a supper.
Where: In the fellowship hall.
When: On Wednesday at 6:30 P.M.
Why: To raise money for new kitchen equipment. If you can go, call me back at 555-5416.

When the person comes home and listens to a jumble of messages and blank spaces, yours will stand out like a jewel.

If you are to order something over the phone, you can use this same outline:

Who: This is Mrs. Paul Stevens and my credit card number is . . .
What: I want to order one pair of Nike tennis shoes, #328, 9B, in blue.
Where: Send them to 6 Beechwood Drive, North Haven, Connecticut.
When: As soon as possible.
Why: I chose to order through you as I've always been satisfied with your quick service.

The order clerk will be thrilled at your concise and positive words and that you had your credit card available.

To communicate a simple message to your family, write:

Who: Tommy
What: I want you to clean
Where: Your room and bath
When: This afternoon
Why: Because we're having company for dinner.

Tommy doesn't have to guess about what his mother wants done or when she needs it completed or why he's doing it. Now we just have to hope he does it!

From these three examples on one basic outline, you can see how helpful this system is to pull your thoughts together and keep you from leaving out important details.

Let's work with a convenient three-point outline: past, present, and future. We used this outline for our last three chapters: Start with the past. Be alert to the present. Journalize for the future.

People can remember so much better when ideas are presented in order. When Barbara Bueler was first working with CLASS, she went to a retreat at Mt. Herman. At dinner a friend announced, "Barbara is learning how to speak and give talks. Tell us about it, Barbara." All eyes turned to Barbara. She swallowed and replied simply, "In the past I used to chatter aimlessly, presently I'm learning all I can about speaking, so that in the future I can share my testimony of hope with others." Barbara was so concise and clear that later several people inquired about her testimony of hope.

So many questions can be answered with the past, present, future outline:

"Why are you eating so little?"
"In the past, I was overweight, so I'm dieting now in order to be thin in the future."

"What are you doing back in school?"
"Back in the fifties I majored in psychology. I'm now getting an M.A. at Cal State so I can become a marriage counselor in the future."

As you begin to think in outline form, your daily communication will improve.

When I discuss marriage problems with a couple, I use the left, center, right outline: "Your marriage started out with both of you in the center, the two became one." I then repeat the problems that have separated them, placing one in left field and one in right. I often take two bottles, two pens, two figurines, the salt and pepper, or whatever's handy to represent the two people, and then move the items around. I show the three alternatives of solving their problem. *She* can go all the way from left field to where he is, expecting nothing in return. *He* can go all the way from right field to her, expecting nothing in return. Or *they* can both come in from the extremes, compromising and forgiving, until they meet in the center. I show them how the Lord can bring them together when they are willing: "If I be lifted up . . . [I] will draw all men unto me."[2] This outline is so simple, yet it keeps us on the track of solving relationship problems. When I move the symbols around, the couple begin to see how far astray they are and what they need to do to come back to the center.

One day Barbara was watching football with her husband, John, when she realized the referee spoke in a brief three-point outline.

She mentioned this revelation to John who said, "Oh, no, he says much more than that." Barbara added with joy, "You just wait until the next foul, and I'll prove it to you." The foul came, and the referee gave his signals as he said: "Illegal holding, Number 65, 10 yards." Barbara showed John this was a what, who, and how outline.

What: Illegal holding
Who: Number 65
How: A ten-yard penalty

As Barbara has learned to see all of life in outlines, she even made one up for my birthday. Since our CLASS theme is, "A word fitly spoken is like an apple of gold," she gave me a candle shaped like an apple and, in addition, Barbara made an acrostic outline from the word *apple*:

We thank you for the:

Appreciation you show us,
Praise you give us,
Pruning you do when we need it,
Love you bestow upon us,
Enduring friendships you have built.

Had she shared these same thoughts without the outline, I would not have remembered them correctly, but by attaching them to a word I knew, she assured my recall.

A few years ago I taught Proverbs 9 as a Bible study. Because I attached it to an appropriate acrostic, I still remember it. Proverbs 9 tells what a wise woman is:

Willing
Intelligent
Stable
Dignified
Open
Mature

Recently Barbara was speaking at a women's retreat. It was time for prayer, but Barbara sensed some ladies were afraid to pray. She did a quick message using another simple outline: problem, result, solution.

Problem: Many women are afraid to pray in public.
Result: They are full of fear and often stay away.
Solution: Write a simple outline in your Bible.

As Barbara explained what to write for those who needed help, she noticed they all opened up their Bibles. She had them jot down for future reference these words:

Opening: Thank You, God, for this beautiful day.
Petition: Please bless each lady here.
Closing: In Jesus' name. Amen.

This may sound too simple to you who are prayer warriors, but it provided a crutch for those who had never dared to pray out loud. They need no longer be afraid.

Just as some people are insecure in how to pray, others don't write thank-you notes because they don't know what to say. Barbara came up with an easy-to-remember outline:

Personal: You're special...
Purpose: Thank you for...
Plan: Keep in touch.

Dear Lauren,

You always know just what to get for a present, and when I saw your gift at the shower last week, I knew from the tasteful wrapping paper and cluster of violets on the top that I would love what was inside.

When I opened the box and saw the white porcelain bunny with those big eyes and pink ears, I was delighted. How thoughtful of you to choose something I can add to my "rabbit collection." Thank you for caring and for coming to the shower.

As soon as Dick and I get settled, we'll have you and Randy over for dinner.

With love and appreciation,

Judy

Do you see how easy it is to write a personal thank-you note? Whenever someone gives you a gift, she deserves a note of thanks which specifically mentions the item. When she has had you for a special dinner, she deserves a note with a mention of some gourmet dish or the new wallpaper in the foyer. The person receiving the note needs to know that you remember the actual gift or what home you were at. Don't ever send a card that is imprinted with "Thank you for the gift," unless you also enclose a specific note.

Don't you love to do things for people who thank you personally and warmly? To be above average, we must always have a grateful spirit for whatever anyone does for us and be sure to let them know it.

It's always special when you get a thank-you note that the person didn't need to write. Stormie Omartian came to our CLASS at the Crystal Cathedral. Although she has her own Christian ministry with her husband, Michael, and has a best-selling album where you exercise to the "Hallelujah Chorus," she took the time to write me this most welcome note:

> Dear Florence, Fred, Marita, and Staff,
> I want to thank you for giving me so much of yourselves during the three days of Basic CLASS in November. The Teaching was a Treasure of Training Touching the heart, Tightening the reins of the mind and Transforming the spirit. (How am I doing?)
> All the material was clear, concise, and valuable. All speakers were *excellent*. I pray that the wealth of your lives continue to enrich millions of others as it has enriched mine.
> Looking forward to seeing you again.
> With much love and blessings,
> Stormie Omartian

Kathy Armstrong came to CLASS and appreciated what an eye-opening experience it was for her personally. Her thank-you note is a classic. It touches on the personal, the purpose, and a plan for the future, plus including some clever outlines:

> Dear Florence,
> The master carpenter used you as an "Instrument" wielding the God given "Tool" of the personalities which cataclysmically "unlocked,

unveiled, and unbridled" the knowledge of God in relationships and He "Set Free" me—the captive.

Thank God for your ministry where He "Resurrected" the person I was, "Resuscitated" the person I am, and "Reconstructed" the person I will be.

Please convey my sincere appreciation to Marita for all her help and hope to see you both in future CLASS seminars and workshops.

Thank you,

Kathy Armstrong

Many years ago when I was in a gift shop I saw a little pillow shaped like a fish with the words "Body and Sole" embroidered on it. Since my friend the late Johnny Green composed the real *Body and Soul*, I bought the pillow and had it mailed to him. The thank-you note he sent me said:

Florence, cherished friend:

I got SUCH a kick and warm giggle from your "BODY AND SOLE" fish! You're pretty darn cute, you are!! How very dear of you, busy as you always are, to think of me and go to the trouble of sending me that adorable "trophy"!! We'll have to find some sort of a special place for "him" ("her"? "it"?).

I hope that this note finds you, Fred and all those dear to you in topmost form in all departments.

My restated thanks are accompanied by Bonnie's and my . . .

Warmest embraces and love,

John Green

We've seen how a simple outline can help in personal thank-you notes, but in business correspondence, order is essential. Leonara wrote, "Beyond speaking, however, I found that by using your outlining principles as a wonderful tool, my business letters are much more effective."

On an airplane I sat next to John Raynesford, an executive with Atlantic-Richfield. Discussing his fascinating career, he summed up the purpose of his visit to each office: "My job is not to solve problems, but to get problems solved while giving others the credit."

His daily life is a two-point outline: problem-solution. This same outline will help you deal with your own problem situations. Let's use a three-point outline, however: problem, alternative, solution. Your daughter didn't make the cheerleading squad, and she is crying over it. Discuss the *problem* and be sympathetic. Go over her attitude *alternatives:*

1. Stay miserable and let everyone know you're a poor sport.
2. Lie and say you didn't want to be on the stupid squad anyway.
3. Admit you're disappointed, but accept it as a growth experience.

As you discuss the alternatives, guide her in choosing the *solution*.

You go to the Church Women's Board Meeting, and they find there is a deficit. You speak up and say, "Our problem is lack of money. Here are some alternatives: 1. We can each chip in $1. 2. We can have a rummage sale; or 3. We can hold a spring luncheon and fashion show. Let's vote on a solution." You are instantly brilliant. You've been able to take a problem, present alternatives, and show them how to choose a solution. It takes so little to be above average!

In *Blow Away the Black Clouds*, I show how to use alternatives in counseling. The understanding of this simple approach will make any one of you able to listen to someone's problem, show alternatives, and guide the person into choosing the correct solution. Always make sure she makes the choice so she can't come back later and blame you.

When I spoke at the School of Prophets at First Baptist Church of Dallas, I heard Dr. W. A. Criswell use a two-point outline that was easy to remember: pastor and people. He gave many excellent examples of how each church needs a pastor and people. Because his outline was simple and clear, I still remember the message and this one example in particular:

If the pastor says he needs $12.55,
the people say the pastor has money on his mind.
If the pastor says he needs $14 million,
the people say the pastor has vision.

Are you beginning to see the value of using outlines in life? God set the world in order, and He so wants us to follow in His footsteps. We've looked at outlining some messages, product orders, notes to children, marriage problems, football games, Bible studies, prayers, thank-you notes, business meetings, counseling, and sermons. Do you see how clear life can be when we think in outline form?

Today practice outlining your telephone conversations.

ADDITIONAL CHALLENGES FOR MEN:

You may have been turned off on outlining when you were in high school, but I hope after reading this chapter, you've seen the value of putting life in order. In business, church, and at home you will find that thinking in outline form is efficient and fun. I've practiced thinking in outlines for so long that I answer questions and converse in outlines. Whatever you ask, I give a 1,2,3, outline and then teach a lesson. My children say, "Where one or two are gathered together, Mother will give a seminar." (Since this is how I earn my living, it's not a bad idea.)

As for thank-you notes, many men think that's the women's responsibility. But what if you have no wife or the one you have won't or can't seem to write any? Do you ignore thanking the people who had you for dinner or gave you a present, or do you do it yourself? Today there are notepapers especially for men in any card store. I am always especially thrilled when I get a thank-you note from a man. Even a FAX can be used to transmit thanks or a quick word of encouragement to a deserving person. If you wish to be way above average, get in the habit of writing notes: giving something personal, stating the purpose, and giving a plan for future relationships. When George Bush was president, he wrote personal notes to world leaders and to ordinary people who did something nice for him. Imagine a handwritten note from the president! Surely, you can do the same.

Outline life.

It takes so little to be above average.

CHAPTER FIFTEEN

Practice
Your Scales

*N*ow that we've seen the value of thinking in an orderly fashion, let's practice. Barbara Bueler calls outlining the "scales of communication." The more hours you practice your scales, the better you will be at the recital.

Sheila Wicks of Fort Worth wrote after attending CLASS:

> Friday morning when Barbara shared on outlining it was all I could do not to stand up and shout. I too had a mental block about outlining from my high school years. A light turned on and I realized in so many areas I was already using outlines. For the rest of the seminar I was like a sponge in every area.

Let's all be like sponges and soak up outlines everywhere we look. Magazine and TV ads are the most obvious material

to work with because they have to say a lot in a brief space
or time.

A Hilton ad is an obvious two-point outline:

> YES we did (change our decor).
> NO we didn't (change our service).

An ad for a Bell System calling card tells:

> How it works.
> How to get yours.

The advertisement for the Ramada Renaissance:

> You deserve it.
> You can afford it.

A Pitney-Bowes dictaphone ad:

> B.D.   A.D.
> (Before Dictaphone)   (After Dictaphone)

Stanford University Nursing Center ad:
> Nursing touches you with hands that:
> Care
> Lead
> Teach
> Touch

How to stop smoking:
> Here's how
> Here's why

What you'll get
Where
When

Do you see how easy it is to spot ready-made outlines in ads? Soon you'll be outlining all of life and communicating clearly. *United* magazine had a glossy spread of pictures showing attractive table settings. The headlines by each picture became the outline:

DINNER

—on the porch
—on the deck
—by the pool
—in the yard
—on the terrace[1]

Brochures frequently have obvious outlines:
International Prayer Fellowship:
Where we began...
Where we are...
Where we've been...
Where we're going...
Arizona Women's Retreat:
Receive
Reflect
Rejoice
Using Air Wisconsin is as easy as:
1 . . .
2 . . .
3 . . .

As you do your scales by outlining ads, brochures, menus (breakfast, lunch, and dinner), and billboards, you will become aware of how much of life is in order.

In *Time*, Hugh Sidey said of the State of the Union message: "It is over hyped by presidents, over anticipated by citizens, and overwhelmed by TV."[2]

An article on John Kennedy reported his being asked, "Do you like being president?" He supposedly answered:

> I have a nice house.
> The pay is good.
> I can walk to work.[3]

Reviews are fun to read. One on a theatrical production on Broadway in New York said of Doug Henning, star of *Magic Show*, "There are three things he cannot do on stage: sing, dance, and act."[4]

As your eye begins to see outlines, your ear will begin to hear them. A TV evangelist said, "We must figure out who we are, what we're doing, and where we're going."

Bo Gritz, Missing in Action (M.I.A.) rescuer, on an early-morning TV show said, "We must solidify our efforts, evaluate our progress, and liberate our prisoners."

Start listening to your pastor with an ear newly tuned and write down his sermon outline. If he doesn't appear to have one, you make one up. I still outline every sermon or speech for practice.

Now you are ready to outline Bible verses for your own edification and for teaching others more clearly:

In John 14:6:
I am the way,
the truth
and the life."

In Acts 2:42:
The early church learned
from the apostles,
fellowshipped together,
shared meals together,
and prayed.

In Acts 6:7:
The word of God contin-
ued to spread.
The number of disciples
grew larger.
A great number of priests
accepted the faith.

In Acts 18:8:
Many people in Corinth
heard the message,
believed, and were baptized.

In Romans 8:28:
All things work together for
good for those
who love the Lord,
who are called according
to His purpose.

In 1 Corinthians 3:6:

I planted the seed,
Apollos watered the plant,
God gave the increase.

In Ephesians 6:10-17:

Put on the armor of God,
have truth for a belt,
put on righteousness for
your breastplate,
add readiness as shoes,
carry faith as a shield,
accept salvation as a helmet,
use the word of God as the
sword.

In Philippians 3:10:

All I want is to
know Christ,
feel the power of his
resurrection,
share in His sufferings,
become like Him.

In 2 Peter 5:2,3:

Church leaders should
be shepherds of the flock,
look after it willingly, work
from a desire to serve,
be examples to the flock.

Do you see how much fun it is to outline Bible verses?
After you have done your scales on verses, you can move on
to chapters and whole books. I have done the chapter and
book of Philemon as a human relations lesson entitled,
"How to Get Along with Difficult People."

I show how Paul, who did not have innate charm or tact,
handled a personality problem by:

compliments	choice
concern	challenge
congratulations	confidence
compromise	conclusion

I have always forced myself to write out an outline and
print up copies of every Bible study I've ever done. I am so
grateful now that I did this, even though I had no mentor to
instruct me, since now I have boxes of outlines to draw from
in speaking and writing.

Remember: When you teach Bible studies,
realize how important it is for you to outline your
message, so *you* will *know* what you're saying, so
they will be able to *remember* it.

As your mind begins to think in outline form, you will
speak and write better, and your new order will pervade the
family. Patsy Clairmont, our court jester, shares that when she
first heard me outlining menus while out to dinner, she didn't
know an outline from an outlaw from an outhouse! But as she
has done her practicing, outlining has become a part of her
family life. One morning Patsy heard a knock at the door. She
opened it, and there stood her seven-year-old Jason.

"What are you doing home?" she asked in surprise.

"I've quit school."

"You've quit school? What brought you to that decision?"

Jason looked up and stated clearly,

> It's too long
> It's too hard
> It's too boring.

Patsy was thrilled and said, "Jason, you've done a three-point outline!" she added, "You've just described life. Get on the bus."

How much more interesting it is to read the paper when you are spotting outlines on every page. One of our CLASS participants gave our staff a toast:

You are all:

> Proud
> Professional
> Prepared
> Positive

Debbie Laurie sent this letter showing us how she had applied the principles of outlining to everyday life:

Dear Florence,

You're right. Our ministry begins first at home. After CLASS, I began to think, how can I motivate my nine- and twelve-year-old daughters to become organized in the morning? Below is my three-point outline:

A. Bath
   1. Toilet
   2. Teeth
   3. Tresses
B. Bedroom
   1. Sheets
   2. Slacks
   3. Shoes
C. Breakfast
   1. Bread
   2. Bacon
   3. Banana

Oh, this is so much fun! Thank you, thank you, thank you!

When in San Antonio, we trained some new staff. One of these women wrote this outlined thank-you note:

Dearest Florence and Staff,
   Please receive my deepest gratitude for the opportunity you gave me this weekend. 1. It has been a privilege to *watch* you, *work* with you, and *wonder* at all God does through you. 2. I wanted you each to know that I thank you for . . .
      risking your
      reputation, in allowing us to
      represent you, CLASS, and our Lord.
   I have *received*
   the *rewards.*

   3. I also *recognize* that in your teaching us to be effective leaders and speakers, you have taught

us to be like Christ. Because who else is the Great Communicator? 4. Thank you for the precious *remembrance* of God's love from each of you.

Speaking in Him,

Joy Chambers

Let's communicate God's love in such a way that everyone will remember what we say.

Today practice looking for outlines in newspaper ads.

ADDITIONAL CHALLENGES FOR MEN:

Even if you automatically outline everything you see, you will have additional challenge and even fun if you practice spotting outlines in ads. Recently in a men's magazine I noticed an ad for Oaktree men's clothes. The full-page ad featured four pictures of well-dressed men. The only print was a line under each picture: Their Time, My Time, Free Time, Over Time, plus one line at the bottom of the page: Oaktree, It's Time.

The VISA card ad sports an outline:

It's in your wallet
It's in your life
It's everywhere you want to be.

Omega fine watches makes it simple:
Time and Tradition

Men's designer shoes by Giorgio Brutini proclaim:
Success is not
Who Has It
It's Who Enjoys It.

When you see a billboard, look for an outline. If there isn't one, make one up and then place a mini message in your head. At one long traffic light you could pick up enough information to write a book.

Remember: Outlining is the scales of communication. So practice your scales.

It takes so little to be above average.

CHAPTER SIXTEEN

Give Your Brain
an Assignment

*C*an you give your brain an assignment at night and wake up with some answers? I had been doing this for years before I realized what was going on in my mind. At bedtime I pray with thanksgiving for the blessings of the day, review with the Lord what I'm facing tomorrow, and ask for His answers on decisions to be made and ideas to be created. One night after I had written an outline for a new message, I realized I needed Scripture to go with the outline. I prayed, "Dear Lord, here's another outline. I need Scripture to go with this. Please give me an answer by morning. I claim Your Psalm 31:2, 'Bow down thine ear to me; deliver me speedily.' In Your precious name. Amen."

When I awoke in the morning, my mind was saying, "Second Timothy, 2 Timothy, 2 Timothy." Picking up my Bible and a pad of paper without getting out of bed, I related the whole book of 2 Timothy to my outline. I soon realized that much of the material for CLASS came from overnight assignments where I need to be delivered "speedily."

As I started teaching other people to give their brains assignments, we came up with results far beyond my expectations. Ladies would come in the following morning crying, "It worked! It worked!" One woman was in tears as she said, "This is the first time in my life I've seen evidence that God's real." One beautiful but sad young lady at our seminar followed our suggestions, and the next morning she came in transformed. "I told my brain to give me a verse that would help my depression. I woke up with John 16:24 on my mind and opened the Bible to find, 'Hitherto have ye asked nothing in my name: ask, and ye shall receive, that your joy may be full.'"

Another girl came in looking tired and asked, "How many nights does it take before you can sleep? I gave my brain an assignment and woke up every two hours to see if I had an answer."

A man said, "I felt foolish putting paper and pen by my bed, but I did it anyway and I woke up with a three-point outline."

Because of the positive results of our "brain assignments," I wrote some directions:

1. Believe giving your brain an assignment will work.
2. Put out paper, pen, and Bible by your bed.
3. Give your brain the assignment.
4. Ask God to answer you "speedily tonight."
5. Write down your first thoughts when you wake up.
6. Thank the Lord for His quick response to your request.

One day as we were talking about the exciting results of "brain assignments," a woman came up with a perfect verse: "I will bless the LORD who has counseled me; indeed, my mind instructs me in the night" (Psalm 16:7 NASB).

Why waste your night? Our bodies need rest, but that unused 90 percent of our mind is happy to work for us into the wee hours of the morning. Start giving your brain assignments and let the Lord instruct you in the night.

Tonight give your brain an assignment.

ADDITIONAL CHALLENGES FOR MEN:

If you apply this plan and begin giving your fertile brain some assignments, the creative results could be worth far more than the price of this book. It is commonly accepted that what your mind is focused on the last thing at night is what your brain plays with while you sleep. If the last thing you see at night is the news and the graphic scenes of the latest murder, you may have a restless night. In contrast, if you commune with the Lord and lay out your needs for the next day, He will use your rest time to create inspired answers. Couldn't you use some motivational messages straight from the Lord? Couldn't this be a new source of intellectual stimulation?

Edward Hennessy, Jr., chairman of Allied Corporation, said, "I absolutely have had good business ideas come to me in a flash—most often at 2 or 3 A.M. I keep a small flashlight and a pad and pencil by my bed so I can record those thoughts and see if they're as brilliant in the morning light as they seem to be in the wee hours."[1]

Don't waste time any longer.

Give your brain an assignment.

It takes so little to be above average.

PART III

It Takes So Little to Look Above Average

CHAPTER SEVENTEEN

Have the Attitude
of a Servant

I t is encouraging that the Bible tells us, "Man looketh on the outward appearance, but the LORD looketh on the heart" (1 Samuel 16:7). Unfortunately, we are dealing with human beings here on earth, and they do make judgments as soon as they take a look at us. You've often heard, "You never get a second chance to make a good first impression," and that is so true. This impression may be made by your clothes or by your attitude. We would like to think that as Christians how we appear or how we act doesn't matter, that everyone sees us through spiritual eyes and accepts us as we are.

Think for a moment. Is there someone you know whose attitude you don't like? She just walks in the room and you cringe. She doesn't have to open her mouth, for just her glance in your direction shows an unacceptable attitude. You judge her before she says a word.

Do you have a friend who's always condemning herself? "My house is too small. I'm so depressed." She slumps on the sofa and sighs. You say to yourself, "Shape up! Stand tall! Start moving!" Her depression depresses you.

Now picture someone who doesn't know how to dress. When your group is going to get together, you wonder what Wanda will wear tonight—will she look even worse than last time? She's probably got a good heart, but who will ever get to know that?

If you have been able to think of even one person who fits the above descriptions, you do form inner opinions based on outside appearances.

You ask, "But doesn't everyone?" Yes, everyone does. That's why we must pay attention to the basics, the ABC's of leadership:

> Attitude
> Bearing
> Clothing

If we notice others, they are probably noticing us. They might judge us on our externals before they ever get to our heart. We see people and instantly communicate to our brain what we think of them.

Even if we are so deep and spiritual that we don't judge a book by its cover, we can't count on many other people having this ability. If we wish to be above average, we must consider our outward appearance, for how we look speaks louder than how we actually may be.

The A of our ABC's is *attitude*. Before we open our mouths, people can sense our attitude. If we are haughty, critical, bored, or depressed, it shows. And when we try to hide our true feelings, people assume we are phonies. When our inner attitude is one of loving concern, we don't have to hand out lollipops to communicate our generous spirit.

In 1983, Great Britain had a memorable election, the most impressive electoral sweep of any political party since 1945. Margaret Thatcher said, "It was a larger victory than I had dared hope for."[1] How did Mrs. Thatcher do it? Even though many of her policies were unpopular, she won by being sincerely herself. She has the attitude of a servant, the bearing of a queen, and the clothes of a leader. Margaret, who grew up living behind her father's store, as I did, worked her way to the top. She gave Britain dignity, and she is sorely missed. She believes that "all power is a trust. We have to use our power wisely and well." *Time* said of her: "The Prime Minister was reelected last week not so much because of specific policies as because of her attitudes. Britons at this point seem to care more about having a strong leader than about exactly where they are led."[2]

What a beautiful statement! What an aim for each one of us: to be chosen because of our attitude, because others can tell when they look at us that we have the ABC's of leadership.

What kind of an attitude appeals to others? When we think of becoming a leader, an administrator, a club president, a chairman, or endeavoring to be a good parent, we too often focus on control, the in-charge feeling. We've often heard, "If I were in charge of this group, we would get something done," or "When I was president, I ran a tight ship." Is leadership "doing and running," or is it, as with Mrs. Thatcher, the right attitude?

When I went in as president of the Women's Club of San Bernardino, I was feared as a religious fanatic by a fringe of the members. Some were afraid I was going to preach or make them join some mystic group. As I prayed for direction, the

Lord led me to 1 Kings 12:7. Solomon had died, and his son Rehoboam was about to be crowned king. He went to his father's advisers, asking what he should do to be an effective ruler. They gave him advice which outlined the attitude needed in any area of leadership:

> Answer all who ask you.
> Speak kindly to all.
> Have the attitude of a servant.

Even though Rehoboam ignored this advice and lost his kingdom, I followed it.

Prayerfully, I planned my presidency with the aim of answering all who asked, of pleasing each member in every way I could. I spoke kindly to all. I developed an attitude of a servant. As the members realized I was always available (I would go to their church luncheons, help in the club kitchen, look at their grandchildren's pictures, or visit them in the hospital), they relaxed and became my friends. When I was nominated for a second term, I won as Mrs. Thatcher had, not for my specific policies but for my attitude. One lady said, "You love us all, and I never saw you get upset with anyone." True leaders will have the attitude of a servant and speak kindly to all.

Today check your attitude, bearing, and clothing to be sure you are in regal apparel.

ADDITIONAL CHALLENGES FOR MEN:

Whether you are leading your family, your church, or a multi-million-dollar business, these principles apply. To succeed in any of these areas, you need to answer all who ask you, not just the questions of the important people. Fred and I were involved in a Christian organization where there was a secret A list and also a B list. List A people were big contributors, and the B's gave a little now and then. Only the top people knew the differentiation. When A's arrived, they were given red-carpet treatment, while the poor B's didn't stand a chance.

According to 1 Kings 12:7, godly leaders answer *all* who ask them and speak kindly to *all*. How easy it is for us to focus on the important people, to fellowship only with those who are like us. Because of this poor example, Fred and I have made a point of looking for the underdog, that person who came alone to the seminar, the one who isn't dressed like the rest, the first-timer at church. Often that person is surprised that we came over to talk to him, and sometimes we even get a note from someone saying, "When you said hello, put your arm around me, told me I had pretty eyes, that brightened up my whole day."

If we want to be above average, we must move beyond our comfort zone, reach out to others, and have the attitude of a servant.

Oswald Chambers says that when we are functioning as true Christians, God knocks "the pretense and the pious pose right out of me. The Holy Spirit reveals that God loved me not because I was loveable, but because it was His nature to do so. Now He says to me, show the same love to others—'*Love as I have loved you.*' I will bring any number of people about you whom you cannot respect, and you must exhibit My Love to them as I have exhibited it to you."[3]

God loves us as we are, and He expects us to do the same to others. God doesn't have a B list.

Have the attitude of a servant.

It takes so little to be above average.

CHAPTER EIGHTEEN

Have the Bearing of a King or Queen

*T*he American people love royalty. We all want to look up to someone. We want an example to follow. When Jimmy Carter went into office, he misread the American public and thought they wanted a leader who was "one of the gang." He emphasized the ordinary, surrounded himself with down-home buddies, and carried his own luggage. There's nothing wrong with doing any of these things, but somehow he didn't come across as presidential. A flurry of articles came out on the qualities of a leader, and we all began to ask ourselves what it was we wanted in a president. When given a new choice, we voted for an actor who had practiced for the presidential role and who surely looked the part. When President Reagan was asked a question on a TV press conference, he stood up straight, gave a confident smile, and said, "I'm glad you asked that question." He may not have known the answer, but he knew his ABC's of leadership. He had the bearing of a king, and Nancy looked like a queen. As you develop your leadership skills, don't let your

Christian humility keep you bowed down in the corner. Stand up straight, walk with confidence, speak with conviction.

Frequently, as I converse with the man next to me on an airplane, he will ask, "What's your business?" I reply, "I'm a Christian speaker."

There is always a pause before, "You don't look like a Christian speaker."

"What does a Christian speaker look like?"

"Well, sort of old and dull, black clothes, hair pulled straight back, no makeup, carrying a Bible, and just home from Africa."

Isn't it a shame we Christians have the reputation of being evangelical frumps? Let's change that image and develop the bearing of royalty. After all, we are children of the King!

As you stand regally before the mirror of life, pretend there's a string on the top of your head being pulled up to heaven. Keep your elbows back and your tummy pulled in. As a king or queen, don't look down on the dummies; rather, smile on the saints.

A leader must have a beautiful bearing, a look of confidence. Make sure before presenting yourself to the court you're put together in such a secure way that you have no doubts draining your demeanor. What happens when you've left home with a button missing from your left sleeve? All day you keep your left hand behind your back and don't dare reach for the coffee. What if there's a run in your panty hose, but you're in a hurry and hope no one will notice? All day you keep standing in corners with your leg against the wall, and when you leave rooms you back out. How nervous will you be if you tie a string around a too-long slip and hope the lace won't show? You'll keep looking for mirrors to check your hem, and you'll have a few friends watching for the fall. When we are insecure on how we're put together, we waste a whole mental track on worry. We can't have the bearing of royalty when we wonder if our subjects will notice:

> We've lost our buttons,
> We're running in the wrong direction, and
> We're held together by string.

For a regal radiance, set your royal train on the right track.

Today stand tall with confidence that you are king or queen for the day.

ADDITIONAL CHALLENGES FOR MEN:

"Are all Christian men wimps?" one single girl asked me. "I haven't been to a church yet that had one decent-looking single man. They're all squirrelly!" Now, men, I have no definition of what a squirrelly man looks like, but this girl was sick of them, whatever they are.

Take a look in the mirror. Would you say you have the bearing of a king? Do you stand up straight? Do you look others in the eye with confidence? Do you have a firm handshake? Do you walk with assurance? Cologne doesn't make a lot of difference if no one gets near enough to smell it.

Regal bearing is not only for single men. Women want to be proud of their husbands, too. They want to look up at you men with admiration. Are you worthy of respect and honor? Think about it. And above all else, don't you dare be squirrelly! Have the bearing of a king.

It takes so little to reign above average.

CHAPTER NINETEEN

Have the Clothing
of a Leader

*T*he Bible tells us our beauty should not depend upon our outward adornment. And yet the virtuous woman of Proverbs 31 was clothed in tapestries of scarlet and in purple silks. She had that look of quiet elegance befitting a queen. How about us?

A lady at our Laguna Beach CLASS said, "I always knew I didn't dress well, but I didn't care. After this week, I still know I don't dress well, but now I care." Caring is being halfway there.

Does it matter what a Christian leader wears? There's no uniform for leadership or requirement for the navy-blue blazer that the "dress for success" look suggests. Yet we should always aim to be one step above average. We don't want to be overdone, but we want to set the pace. When I lived in Connecticut and was president of the League of Women Voters, the level of dress for the meetings and teas was tweed suits and flat shoes. They all looked as if they had been tramping through the moors in Scotland. I could have headed for the herringbones, but instead I continued to wear my more-feminine suits and dresses. Slowly, the other women began to change. By the end of the term, everyone came dressed up.

Francine Jackson attends Toastmasters in Evergreen, Colorado, the mountain community where she lives. Francine always dresses tastefully in simple elegance, even in the mountains. When she first began attending meetings, the women were in jeans and hiking boots, the men in flannel shirts. Asked to speak on some topic she felt strongly about, Francine titled her message "Let's Dress Up." From that time on, she noticed a difference in how they all looked. Now they do "dress up." Given a living example, people will rise to be above average.

Your aim should be to have a unified or "put-together" look. The viewer should see you and not your clothes. One night we took some CLASS ladies to a department store known for its classy clothes at budget prices. We found one dress that was a perfect bad example. The background was black-and-white zebra stripes, and right across the bosom was a large zebra head with an open mouth and big eyes. It looked right out of the ark! Scattered across the stripes, here and there, were large flowers in bright orange and hot pink. And to give the final touch, the dress had rhinestone buttons.

Since I will give a mini-seminar anywhere, I called the women over and showed them how not to dress. Francine found some other bad examples, and we held each one in front of us and asked, "When you look at me, what do you see? If the answer is 'zebras, stripes, or flowers,' we must be a little too loud."

Try on your clothes and ask yourself, "What do I see?" If you have an outfit that complements your natural color, if no part of it stands out, and if your shoes blend with the total look, you are probably all right.

Each one of us is different, and we should aim to wear the colors and styles that do the very best for us, not ones that looked good on our friends.

When God appointed Aaron to be the high priest, the spiritual leader, He said, "Make special clothes for Aaron, to indicate his separation to God—beautiful garments that will lend dignity to his work" (Exodus 28:2 TLB). Begin to build a wardrobe of special clothes that will add dignity to your work.

The ABC's of leadership give us some simple guidelines. Have the:

> Attitude of a servant
> Bearing of a queen
> Clothing of a leader

The following letter sums up the attributes of leadership:

> Dear Florence,
> I attended your CLASS seminar in Detroit. I found it to be entertaining and informative. I was challenged in many areas. I felt better about myself as I left the seminar. I learned one very important lesson in an area I have struggled with for years. The prim and proper person was always someone I resented. I had a built in prejudice against them. I felt the walls coming down each day I was around you. On Thursday when you explained the importance of always maintaining a servant spirit, I knew you meant it because the night before at the restaurant you had exhibited just that as you took time at our table answering

our questions and sharing with us. I couldn't believe a person of your status was spending all that time with us.

As I thought about your ABC's of becoming a quality leader/speaker, I realized my thoughts had changed. When you said "A" was attitude, I at first felt it was an attitude that creates an *air* of snobbishness. Now I see it as an attitude that creates an *atmosphere* of love.

When you said "B" was for bearing, I saw a bearing determined to *brag* about self. Now I see bearing as determined to *boast* only of Christ.

When you said "C" was for clothing, I saw clothing which exhibited *conceit* over my importance. Now I see it as clothing that exhibits *confidence* in the God we serve.

Thank you for helping to remove my prejudices. I will begin to work on the "so little it takes to be above average." Thank you for following through on a vision that will help those desiring to improve their speaking in order that the gospel be presented with the highest quality possible.

Love,
Dana Ryan

When you act like a leader, walk like a leader, and look like a leader, people will begin to follow you.

Today take an extra minute to look at yourself in the mirror and check your attitude, bearing, and clothing.

ADDITIONAL CHALLENGES FOR MEN:

It is so much easier for you to dress well than it is for women. A few sport coats with coordinating pants, white shirts, and an assortment of neckties, and you're set for the season. Most men have little trouble dressing for work. You know what's expected, and you dress accordingly. The area where I find men are often confused is in social situations. Even if you don't care, realize your wife desperately wants you to look good. She wants to be proud of you, and she usually knows what her friends' husbands are going to wear. I always feel sorry for the lady who apologizes to me for her husband's appearance. "I told him all the men would be wearing ties, and he said he didn't care. No one could make him wear a tie at night."

Men, please listen and wear what's the norm for the occasion. Don't show up in a Hawaiian-print sport shirt, as if you just stepped off a cruise ship, when the other men are in suits. And if you happen to have a leftover polyester leisure suit, rush it quickly to the Salvation Army.

Have the clothing of a leader.

It takes so little to be above average.

PART IV

*It Takes So Little
to Understand
Others Above
Average*

CHAPTER TWENTY

Understand Yourself and Others

I n the 25-plus years that Fred and I have been teaching and writing on the four basic personalities, we have seen thousands of lives changed. To know that their spouse was born with a certain personality that's not like theirs and that different isn't wrong relieves people from thinking that their marriage is a mistake. Once Fred and I realized that my strengths filled in his weaknesses and that his strengths filled in my empty spots, we stopped trying to change each other and began to accept each other as we were created by a God who loves us.

The theory of the four personalities has been around for over 2000 years, and it still serves as a simple tool for us to do what Scripture commands: "Let a man examine himself" (1 Corinthians 11:28). The first one is the Popular Sanguine, born to have fun, eager for attention, the life of the party. I was thrilled to find myself in this category until I saw this personality's weaknesses: wanting to play (or shop) rather than work, talking too much, and not letting the truth stand in the way of a good story.

Fred was the Perfect Melancholy. If it's worth doing, it's worth doing right. This person was born with perfection on his mind, loves to analyze and schedule his life and the lives of others, and needs sensitivity and silence once in a while. The negatives of this personality type are putting too much emphasis on perfection, getting depressed when things don't go right, and having no flexibility or tolerance for those who want to wing it through life.

Once Fred and I got a handle on this, we could see our problems laid out before us. I wanted to live free as a breeze and have fun, while he wanted each day scheduled and thought just plain fun was a waste of time. We had spent years trying to change each other, instead of accepting our natures and enjoying our differences as we do now.

The third personality is the Powerful Choleric who is the born leader, who takes charge of every situation (even when not asked), and who wants obedience, loyalty, and appreciation for all the great works he or she has done for you. This person works more and harder than all other types, and expects you to do the same. This powerful person wants everything done his way *now*, and looks down on lazy people. This type often becomes a workaholic and avoids any activity that is not rewarding or accomplishing some purpose.

Fred and I found that not only were we opposites (Sanguine and Melancholy), but we were also both part Choleric, wanting to be in control. This mutual take-charge attitude had also led to conflict since I wanted to be in charge and have fun, and Fred wanted to be in charge and keep things serious. No wonder we had grown further apart each year! What an eye-opening experience it was when we could see our problems laid out clearly before us and begin to accept each other as we were made to be.

The fourth type is the Peaceful Phlegmatic. Neither of us had any of the sweet, gentle spirit of the Phlegmatic. This person wants to please, avoids any kind of conflict or confrontation, and wants to be loved for his inner strength and not because of how much he produces in a given day. This person hates the question, "What did you get done today?" The Phlegmatic is the most well-liked, inoffensive person ever created, but often appears lazy, disinterested, and indecisive, especially to the Powerful Choleric.

As you read these personalities over, you can probably see yourself, your mate, your family members and coworkers. Understand that we were all created with different inborn personalities. The sooner you see this, the faster you will cease your vain striving to make others like you. This will be a freeing, relaxing experience and make you a lot easier to live with.

In my book *Personality Plus*, I give many humorous stories on the different types of personalities. *Your Personality Tree* deals with personalities in your family background; *Personality Puzzle* applies the principles to the workplace; *Put Power in Your Personality* deals with leadership skills; and *Raising Christians Not Just Children* shows how each kind of parent deals with each kind of child.

In this book I want you to see the value of understanding yourself and others so that you can use this simple analytical tool to move you above average and whet your appetite for further study. I want your life and relationships to change as ours have. I've included at the end of this chapter the Personality Profile, and the Personality Scoring Sheet for your use and your family's edification. You will all enjoy doing the Profile and discussing it together. Also, I have included four simple self-explanatory charts to give you the basics and help you apply the personality principles in your home life and your business.

Today take the Personality Profile and see what kind of a nature you have.

ADDITIONAL CHALLENGES FOR MEN:

So often I have women tell me that when they go home from a Personality Plus seminar and share excitedly with their husbands about their new understanding, the men turn them off immediately. "I don't fit in one of those little boxes." "This is too simple." "I did something like this at work, and it didn't help any." "That's okay for you women, but don't bother me with your little games."

Words like these are so devastating and wipe out much of the new understanding that would greatly benefit the entire family. I am hopeful that you men will have a more accepting attitude and will consider it a family blessing to take the profile and discuss your differences, pointing out that different is good, not bad. We have seen so many transformed families when the father took the leadership to open up the family evaluation.

Wouldn't you like to be understood by your family? Wouldn't you like them to look forward to your return each day? Wouldn't you like to have them respect and not nag each other? The personalities provide you with a simple, effective tool by which you may all learn to understand yourself and others.

It takes so little to be above average.

Personality
Profile

PERSONALITY PROFILE

DIRECTIONS: In *each* of the following rows of *four words across*, place an X in front of the *one* word that most often applies to you. Continue through all forty lines. Be sure each number is marked. If you are not sure of which word "most applies," ask a spouse or a friend, and think of what your answer would have been *when you were a child.* (Note: Definitions of test words are found in the Appendix.)

STRENGTHS

#				
1	X Adventurous	___ Adaptable	___ Animated	___ Analytical
2	___ Persistent	___ Playful	___ Persuasive	___ Peaceful
3	___ Submissive	___ Self-sacrificing	___ Sociable	X Strong-willed
4	___ Considerate	___ Controlled	X Competitive	___ Convincing
5	___ Refreshing	___ Respectful	___ Reserved	___ Resourceful
6	___ Satisfied	___ Sensitive	X Self-reliant	___ Spirited
7	X Planner	___ Patient	___ Positive	___ Promoter
8	___ Sure	___ Spontaneous	___ Scheduled	___ Shy
9	___ Orderly	___ Obliging	X Outspoken	___ Optimistic
10	X Friendly	___ Faithful	___ Funny	___ Forceful
11	X Daring	___ Delightful	___ Diplomatic	___ Detailed
12	___ Cheerful	___ Consistent	___ Cultured	X Confident
13	___ Idealistic	X Independent	___ Inoffensive	___ Inspiring
14	___ Demonstrative	___ Decisive	X Dry humor	___ Deep
15	___ Mediator	___ Musical	___ Mover	___ Mixes easily
16	X Thoughtful	___ Tenacious	___ Talker	___ Tolerant
17	___ Listener	___ Loyal	X Leader	X Lively
18	X Contented	___ Chief	___ Chartmaker	___ Cute
19	___ Perfectionist	___ Pleasant	___ Productive	___ Popular
20	___ Bouncy	X Bold	___ Behaved	___ Balanced

WEAKNESSES

#				
21	Blank	[X] Bashful	Brassy	Bossy
22	Undisciplined	Unsympathetic	Unenthusiastic	[X] Unforgiving
23	Reticent	Resentful	Resistant	[X] Repetitious
24	Fussy	Fearful	Forgetful	Frank
25	Impatient	Insecure	Indecisive	[X] Interrupts
26	Unpopular	Uninvolved	Unpredictable	Unaffectionate
27	[X] Headstrong	Haphazard	Hard-to-please	Hesitant
28	Plain	Pessimistic	[X] Proud	Permissive
29	Angered easily	Aimless	[X] Argumentative	Alienated
30	Naive	Negative attitude	[X] Nervy	Nonchalant
31	Worrier	Withdrawn	[X] Workaholic	Wants credit
32	Too sensitive	Tactless	Timid	Talkative
33	Doubtful	Disorganized	Domineering	Depressed
34	Inconsistent	[X] Introvert	Intolerant	Indifferent
35	Messy	Moody	Mumbles	[X] Manipulative
36	[X] Slow	Stubborn	[X] Show-off	Skeptical
37	[X] Loner	Lord-over-others	[X] Lazy	Loud
38	Sluggish	Suspicious	Short-tempered	[X] Scatterbrained
39	Revengeful	Restful	Reluctant	Rash
40	Compromising	[X] Critical	Crafty	Changeable

NOW TRANSFER ALL YOUR X's TO THE SCORE SHEET AND ADD UP YOUR TOTALS

PERSONALITY SCORING SHEET

STRENGTHS

	SANGUINE POPULAR	CHOLERIC POWERFUL	MELANCHOLY PERFECT	PHLEGMATIC PEACEFUL
1	Animated	Adventurous	Analytical	Adaptable
2	Playful	Persuasive	Persistent	Peaceful
3	Sociable	Strong-willed	Self-sacrificing	Submissive
4	Convincing	Competitive	Considerate	Controlled
5	Refreshing	Resourceful	Respectful	Reserved
6	Spirited	Self-reliant	Sensitive	Satisfied
7	Promoter	Positive	Planner	Patient
8	Spontaneous	Sure	Scheduled	Shy
9	Optimistic	Outspoken	Orderly	Obliging
10	Funny	Forceful	Faithful	Friendly
11	Delightful	Daring	Detailed	Diplomatic
12	Cheerful	Confident	Cultured	Consistent
13	Inspiring	Independent	Idealistic	Inoffensive
14	Demonstrative	Decisive	Deep	Dry humor
15	Mixes easily	Mover	Musical	Mediator
16	Talker	Tenacious	Thoughtful	Tolerant
17	Lively	Leader	Loyal	Listener
18	Cute	Chief	Chartmaker	Contented
19	Popular	Productive	Perfectionist	Pleasant
20	Bouncy	Bold	Behaved	Balanced
Subtotals				

WEAKNESSES

#				
21	Brassy	Bossy	Bashful ✓	Blank
22	Undisciplined	Unsympathetic ✓	Unforgiving	Unenthusiastic
23	Repetitious	Resistant ✓	Resentful	Reticent
24	Forgetful ✓	Frank	Fussy	Fearful
25	Interrupts	Impatient ✓	Insecure	Indecisive
26	Unpredictable ✓	Unaffectionate ✓	Unpopular	Uninvolved
27	Haphazard	Headstrong ✓	Hard-to-please	Hesitant
28	Permissive	Proud	Pessimistic	Plain
29	Angered easily	Argumentative ✓	Alienated	Aimless
30	Naive	Nervy ✓	Negative attitudes ✓	Nonchalant
31	Wants credit ✓	Workaholic ✓	Withdrawn ✓	Worrier
32	Talkative	Tactless	Too sensitive ✓	Timid
33	Disorganized	Domineering	Depressed ✓	Doubtful
34	Inconsistent	Intolerant	Introvert ✓	Indifferent ✓
35	Messy	Manipulative	Moody	Mumbles
36	Show-off ✓	Stubborn	Skeptical ✓	Slow
37	Loud	Lord-over-others ✓	Loner	Lazy
38	Scatterbrained	Short tempered ✓	Suspicious ✓	Sluggish
39	Restless	Rash	Revengeful	Reluctant
40	Changeable	Crafty ✓	Critical ✓	Compromising
Subtotals				
GRAND TOTALS	4	23	10	3

STRENGTHS

	SANGUINE-POPULAR	CHOLERIC-POWERFUL
E M O T I O N S	Appealing personality Talkative, storyteller Life of the party Good sense of humor Memory for color Physically holds on to listener Emotional and demonstrative Enthusiastic and expressive Cheerful and bubbling over Curious Good on stage Wide-eyed and innocent Lives in the present Changeable disposition Sincere at heart Always a child	Born leader Dynamic and active Compulsive need for change Must correct wrongs Strong-willed and decisive Unemotional Not easily discouraged Independent and self-sufficient Exudes confidence Can run anything
W O R K	Volunteers for jobs Thinks up new activities Looks great on the surface Creative and colorful Has energy and enthusiasm Starts in a flashy way Inspires others to join Charms others to work	Goal oriented Sees the whole picture Organizes well Seeks practical solutions Moves quickly to action Delegates work Insists on production Makes the goal Stimulates activity Thrives on opposition
F R I E N D S	Makes friends easily Loves people Thrives on compliments Seems exciting Envied by others Doesn't hold grudges Apologizes quickly Prevents dull moments Likes spontaneous activities	Has little need for friends Will work for group activity Will lead and organize Is usually right Excels in emergencies

STRENGTHS

MELANCHOLY-PERFECT	PHLEGMATIC-PEACEFUL
Deep and thoughtful Analytical Serious and purposeful Genius prone Talented and creative Artistic or musical Philosophical and poetic Appreciative of beauty Sensitive to others Self-sacrificing Conscientious Idealistic	Low-key personality Easygoing and relaxed Calm, cool, and collected Patient, well balanced Consistent life Quiet, but witty Sympathetic and kind Keeps emotions hidden Happily reconciled to life All-purpose person
Schedule oriented Perfectionist, high standards Detail conscious Persistent and thorough Orderly and organized Neat and tidy Economical Sees the problems Finds creative solutions Needs to finish what he starts Likes charts, graphs, figures, lists	Competent and steady Peaceful and agreeable Has administrative ability Mediates problems Avoids conflicts Good under pressure Finds the easy way
Makes friends cautiously Content to stay in background Avoids causing attention Faithful and devoted Will listen to complaints Can solve other's problems Deep concern for other people Moved to tears with compassion Seeks ideal mate	Easy to get along with Pleasant and enjoyable Inoffensive Good listener Dry sense of humor Enjoys watching people Has many friends Has compassion and concern

WEAKNESSES

	SANGUINE-POPULAR	CHOLERIC-POWERFUL
E M O T I O N S	Compulsive talker Exaggerates and elaborates Dwells on trivia Can't remember names Scares others off Too happy for some Has restless energy Egotistical Blusters and complains Naive, gets taken in Has loud voice and laugh Controlled by circumstances Gets angry easily Seems phony to some Never grows up	Bossy Impatient Quick-tempered Can't relax Too impetuous Enjoys controversy and arguments Won't give up when losing Comes on too strong Inflexible Is not complimentary Dislikes tears and emotions Is unsympathetic
W O R K	Would rather talk Forgets obligations Doesn't follow through Confidence fades fast Undisciplined Priorities out of order Decides by feelings Easily distracted Wastes time talking	Little tolerance for mistakes Doesn't analyze details Bored by trivia May make rash decisions May be rude or tactless Manipulates people Demanding of others End justifies the means Work may become his god Demands loyalty in the ranks
F R I E N D S	Hates to be alone Needs to be center stage Wants to be popular Looks for credit Dominates conversations Interrupts and doesn't listen Answers for others Fickle and forgetful Makes excuses Repeats stories	Tends to use people Dominates others Decides for others Knows everything Can do everything better Is too independent Possessive of friends and mate Can't say, "I'm sorry" May be right, but unpopular

WEAKNESSES

MELANCHOLY-PERFECT	PHLEGMATIC-PEACEFUL
Remembers the negatives Moody and depressed Enjoys being hurt Has false humility Off in another world Low self-image Has selective hearing Self-centered Too introspective Guilt feelings Persecution complex Tends to hypochondria	Unenthusiastic Fearful and worried Indecisive Avoids responsibility Quiet will of iron Selfish Too shy and reticent Too compromising Self-righteous
Not people oriented Depressed over imperfections Chooses difficult work Hesitant to start projects Spends too much time planning Prefers analysis to work Self-deprecating Hard-to-please Standards often too high Deep need for approval	Not goal oriented Lacks self-motivation Hard to get moving Resents being pushed Lazy and careless Discourages others Would rather watch
Lives through others Insecure socially Withdrawn and remote Critical of others Holds back affection Dislikes those in opposition Suspicious of people Antagonistic and vengeful Unforgiving Full of contradictions Skeptical of compliments	Dampens enthusiasm Stays uninvolved Is not exciting Indifferent to plans Judges others Sarcastic and teasing Resists change

How To Understand Others By Understanding Yourself

POPULAR SANGUINE

Basic Desire:
Have Fun

Emotional Needs:
Attention
Affection
Approval
Acceptance

Controls By:
Charm

LEAD
Extroverted • Optimistic • Outspoken

POWERFUL CHOLERIC

Basic Desire:
Have Control

Emotional Needs:
Loyalty
Sense of control
Appreciation
Credit for work

Controls By:
Threat of Anger

PLAY
Witty • Easygoing • Not Goal Oriented

WORK
Decisive • Organized • Goal Oriented

PEACEFUL PHLEGMATIC

Basic Desire:
Have Peace

Emotional Needs:
Peace and quiet
Feeling of worth
Lack of stress
Respect

Controls By:
Procrastination

ANALYZE
Introverted • Pessimistic • Soft-Spoken

PERFECT MELANCHOLY

Basic Desire:
Have Perfection

Emotional Needs:
Sensitivity
Support
Space
Silence

Controls By:
Threat of Moods

Meet Other People's Needs

*I*n the previous chapter we looked at the four personality types so we could begin to understand ourselves and others. We need to realize that we are all born with a distinct personality, and our aim is to function in our strengths and not just slog through life in our weaknesses.

As we begin to see the differences in ourselves and others, we become less critical and more accepting of people who are nothing like us. We don't use our knowledge to become amateur psychologists, to pin labels on people, or as an excuse for our continued bad behavior. We use this information as a tool to help us understand our own reactions to the situations of life and to improve our relationship skills with other people.

With each type of personality there are strengths, weaknesses, and emotional needs. Most of us would be willing to meet others' needs if we only knew what they needed. They can't express their needs in simple terms, and we can't figure out what's wrong with them. We're going to do a simple exercise that will instantly change the way you handle other people. We all know that in business, people skills are often more important than technical knowledge. Yet many times we just can't figure out those other people.

Popular Sanguine

Let's start with the Popular Sanguine. Think of some person you know who is outgoing, optimistic, talkative, wide-eyed, excitable, and colorful. This person loves to be the center of attention and the life of the party. Write down the name of this person or persons.

Would you like to get along better with these individuals and have them think you are the greatest person in the world?

Then meet their emotional needs. What are they?

1. *Attention*—From the time the Sanguines were little, they have been craving attention. That's why they have loud voices and wear bright clothes. Parents may have been too busy or felt that paying attention to children's desires might spoil them. When these needs aren't met as children, the emotions don't mature, and we find an adult Sanguine desperate for someone who will listen, laugh, and nod in affirmation. Can you do this for the person you have in mind?

2. *Approval*—For this kind of person, approval is the food of life. Without it, they never really grow up. No matter what they do, they desire someone to say, "That's great. Keep it up." They will work into the night if they receive enough approval. Do you encourage this Sanguine, or do you feel he should do his duty without your praise? Without constant approval, Sanguines accomplish little, and with constant criticism, they do even less.

3. *Acceptance*—For Sanguines the need for acceptance and belonging is stronger than in any of the other personalities. From childhood on they have received the message that if they ever grow up and get serious, quit playing games, and accomplish something, they might be acceptable. They are in desperate need to hear that they are acceptable—not as they might someday become if they try hard enough, but now.

If you wish to get along with the Sanguines in your life, let them know that from here on you will give them undivided attention, that you approve of their abilities and actions, and that you accept them as they are today. You will be surprised at their change of attitude toward you.

Perfect Melancholy

Think now of the opposite personality, the Perfect Melancholy. Write down those individuals who come to your mind who are deep, thoughtful, introspective, analytical, intelligent, philosophical perfectionists. This person's motto is "If it's worth doing, it's worth doing right," and he or she gets easily depressed when things go wrong.

Their emotional needs are all inner needs, while the Sanguines' are outer.

1. *Sensitivity*—The Melancholy spends a lifetime trying to find someone who will say, "I understand." My melancholy husband used to say, "If you really loved me, you'd know what I'm thinking." I had no idea what was locked up inside, and I was insensitive to his needs. The Melancholy is easily hurt by the humorous put-downs of the Sanguines who think they're funny, and the Melancholies long for someone who seems to care about their inner needs.

2. *Support*—Because Melancholies drop down so easily, they need someone around who will lift them up in a gentle way. They do not respond well to the loud, overly positive person who declares, "Let's all cheer up and be happy!" They want someone to wait patiently until they're ready to share their inner feelings and hurts. Sometimes this can be a long wait. Melancholies don't need constant praise as Sanguines do, but they like people who notice their depth and are gently supportive.

3. *Space and Silence*—The Sanguine needs people and action, but the Melancholy gets drained by too many people and too much action. They like to retreat, find their own space, and sit quietly to analyze life. Sometimes my melancholy grandson will get up from a family dinner party and go to his room. The volume and fun of the group has become too much, and he needs a rest. Because we understand his personality, we don't worry and run after him; we know he needs some space to himself and some silence instead of noise.

If you wish to please Melancholies, talk softly and be sensitive to their fragile emotions. Don't come on too strong or try to jolly them up. Try to understand their feelings. Don't expect fun and games or even noticeable response to your humor. Respect their space and realize that for them silence is golden.

The other two personalities are not quite as emotionally needy, but they will respond to you in opposite ways.

Powerful Choleric

The Powerful Choleric is the born leader who takes charge of every situation and feels responsible to guide all the incompetents in life. They are strong-willed, controlling, and easily become workaholics. They stay positive as long as things are going their way but get angry quickly when someone crosses them. Their emotional needs are simple and obvious. Write down any of these people whom you know.

1. *Appreciation*—Because the Cholerics are working circles around other people, they want recognition for their superhuman efforts. "I can't believe how much you've done!" "I've never seen anyone who could accomplish so much in a given day!" These are words that will endear you to Cholerics, who are hopeful you noticed that they are the only ones really working around here. They are constantly teaching and training those around them (whether or not they were asked) and get upset if people don't respond in appreciation for all they've done.

2. *Loyalty*—Not only do they want appreciation, but they also expect undying devotion for their contribution. If you don't praise them or leave because you can't work with them or for them, they will be innocently baffled and say, "I can't believe they've left after all I have done for them." With the Choleric personality, you are either with them or against them. There is no middle ground. Interestingly, these black-and-white individuals usually marry the Peaceful Phlegmatic who can't make a quick decision and who sees all life as gray. The Phlegmatic hopes the Choleric will slow down and rest, and the Choleric is waiting impatiently for the Phlegmatic to get up and do something. When the Choleric comes home from work, his question is, "What did you get done today?"

If you are dealing with Cholerics, remember they are the great achievers of life, but they want you to tell them you've noticed. They want to hear words of loyalty, and they become suspicious and angry at the hint of an insurrection. While the Sanguines need approval of how cute and adorable they are and how well they dress, the Cholerics want praise for how much work they have done. So notice the completed projects and let the Cholerics know you are loyal and devoted. They will be thrilled with your discernment.

Peaceful Phlegmatic

Now for the easiest person to get along with of them all: the Peaceful Phlegmatic. They want to avoid trouble and controversy and will go along with just about anything to keep peace. They are stable, dependable, unemotional, balanced, middle-of-the-road people who keep their emotions hidden. My phlegmatic mother used to say with pride, "No one ever knows what I'm really thinking." And we didn't.

Because Phlegmatics don't have the volatile emotions of the other three personalities, they don't get the attention the others demand. As children, they stayed out of trouble and didn't insist on praise or even being noticed. While Sanguines take the fun way, Melancholies the right way, Cholerics the "do it my way," Phlegmatics take the easy way. Easy does it. Do you know a few Phlegmatics. Have you wondered why they were so quiet? Jot down the names of any you can think of.

1. *Respect*—Rodney Dangerfield complains, "I don't get no respect." That's what Phlegmatics are looking for: respect and honor for who they are and not for how much they do or how cute they look. They have been ignored so much in the past and overlooked so often for plum positions that they

long for someone who will love them as they are. Usually, Phlegmatics are single-minded, and as children they need parents who will help them find their niche. As adults, if they are in the right place, they will work long and hard on their projects, not looking to the left or right. When they go home, having given their all at the office, they often collapse in front of the television, causing the Cholerics in the family to brand them as lazy. This appellation saps what little energy they have left and causes them to ponder, "Doesn't anyone like me for me?"

2. *Peace*—The Phlegmatics have a unique talent: They can shut out all the turmoil around them and retreat to another world, a never-never land of peace. Realizing that peace and quiet are essentials for the Phlegmatic's emotional stability, perhaps we could help. We could give a Phlegmatic child a quiet room, or at least not burden him with a bossy Choleric brother who will stir up trouble. As a mate, we can appreciate the sweet and gentle spirit and be grateful for the balance the Phlegmatic provides in a sea of turmoil. In business, we need to supply the Phlegmatic with a peaceful corner away from the other workers if we wish maximum achievement.

Don't put Phlegmatics down by asking, "When are you going to get up and do something?" Give them respect and a modicum of peace, and they'll never give you a bit of trouble.

As you understand the emotional needs of each person, make a pledge to attempt to meet them. Look back over the names you've jotted down and see if you can handle them differently in the future. The secret to success in human relationships is to deal with others not on the basis of your own personality's needs, but by understanding theirs. What a difference this could make!

Today jot down those names and reflect on the needs of others.

ADDITIONAL CHALLENGES FOR MEN:

Everything in this chapter on emotional needs is especially important for you in dealing with your wife, your family, and your business. For those of you who are divorced, you may see for the first time why your marriage failed, what your wife needed that you didn't provide, what you wanted that she didn't understand. You men may suddenly see why you get along with one child and can't stand another. You may know that the Sanguine wants attention and approval for every trivial pursuit, the Melancholy longs to be understood and needs a respite from family activities, the Choleric needs praise for achievements so he'll keep doing more and more, and the Phlegmatic just wants to hear, "I love you whether or not you did anything today."

If you haven't done it, go back and jot down names of the different personalities you know and then decide what you can do to meet their emotional needs and make a positive change in all of your lives.

Meet other people's needs starting today.

It takes so little to be above average.

PART V

It Takes So Little to Lead Above Average

CHAPTER TWENTY-TWO

Give an Announcement

Dull announcements following each other in single file have led many clubs and church groups over the cliff of monotony into the valley of poor attendance. Unfortunately, once a club is in the valley, it is difficult to renew its membership. In order to keep any group alive, those who feel led to make announcements should first ask themselves two questions: "What am I trying to say?" and "Does anyone need to hear it?"

If no further instructions were given, the first question would eliminate the ennui felt when chairmen stumble up totally unprepared, shuffle through stacks of papers, and, for lack of a message, end up reviewing what everyone wore at the last meeting. Even if there is something to say, the chairman should ask himself if anyone needs to hear it. If a chairman has objectively answered yes to these two questions, he or she should proceed to the "Four Commandments of Announcements":

1. Make it clear.
2. Make it positive.
3. Make it brief.
4. Make it complimentary.

Make It Clear

Many times a chairman muddles through her announcement and mutters her words in such a way that no one is quite sure what she was talking about by the time she sits down. This confusion promotes murmuring in the ranks, and the president can hardly regain control as the debate goes on. "Was it for Tuesday or Wednesday?" "January or February?" "Was the money for scholarships or tea chairs?" The simple solution for clear announcements is to follow the "Five Journalistic W's": who, what, where, when, and why.

> *Who* is sponsoring the activity?
> *What* is its plan and purpose?
> *Where* will it be?
> *When* is it being held?
> *Why* is it important to attend?

For example:

Who: The Bible-study section led by Mrs.
        Eason is
What: having an open meeting for all club
        members
Where: here in the clubhouse
When: on Thursday morning at 9:30 A.M.
Why: Mrs. Eason will teach from the book of

Philippians and cover a subject we all need to hear: "How to Have Joy in Adverse Circumstances."

• • •

Who: The Scholarship Committee chaired by Hazelle Howard

What: will put on the 18th Annual Scholarship Luncheon

Where: at the Arrowhead Country Club

When: on Wednesday, February 18, at noon.

Why: The proceeds will go to nursing students at Valley College. Knowing the need there is for qualified nurses, I am sure you will want to support this event.

• • •

Who: Pastor Maxwell will begin

What: a six-week discipleship training for men

Where: in the pastor's study

When: each Saturday morning, beginning April 11,

Why: to lift the level of male leadership in the church.

Each one of these announcements is simple and clear. If more information is needed, add it, but make sure you have included the essentials. The five W's give a guideline and take the rambling factor out of announcements.

Make It Positive

It is very difficult to instill enthusiasm for any activity if the speaker is dwelling on the negatives: "There's very little to say about next month's speaker"; "I'm new in this job, and last year's chairman didn't give me a thing to go on"; "With all the problems I've had dumped on me, there's no way I could do this job right"; "No one in this club has ever had any interest in mental health." After opening lines like these, the chairman would have a difficult time finding volunteers to help. The rejection proves that this leadership position is hopeless, so the chairman retreats into obscurity until next month, emerging to try hopelessly again. Whatever your announcement is about, make it positive. If there is nothing good to say about your program, perhaps it should be disbanded. On the other hand, an enthusiastic approach, plus some free food, may be all that the mental health committee needs to get rolling.

For example:

> This is my first year as chairman of mental health, and I am sincerely challenged by the needs in this community. I have prepared a list of available opportunities for volunteer help, and I will present these openings for assistance at my home next Tuesday at noon. I will be serving a chicken salad luncheon with chocolate cream pie for dessert. Now, will all of you interested in joining my committee please raise your hands so I'll know how much lunch to prepare?

It is amazing how many women will join at the thought of an exciting meal or the opportunity to visit a home of importance.

When I was membership chairman of the League of Women Voters, I asked a lady who owned a beautiful home overlooking a lake if we could use her home for the membership tea. After I announced that the tea would be held at a home everyone had always wanted to see, one of the largest crowds ever attending a membership tea turned out.

When my husband was president of the Rotary Club, one of the men stood up to get volunteers to take exchange students into their homes for two weeks. He started by saying, "Probably most of you won't want to do this, but we've got ten foreign exchange students we've got to put somewhere. The last time we did this my wife vowed, 'Never again!' but you'll no doubt have better luck than we did."

Doesn't that make you want to take some teen who perhaps doesn't speak English into your home and hope he doesn't upset your routine and steal your silver? If we want volunteers to volunteer, we've got to emphasize the positive and not dwell on the negatives.

Make It Brief

While some members will not stand up to second a motion, there are always plenty of announcers who tend to ramble on. The topic of the garden committee chairman's report is lost in a torrent of trivia: "You'll never know what trouble I had to go to for these flowers on the tea table today. I started a month ago by calling Helen. She's the one that lives on Lorna Lane next door to Dr. Abbott. She has 200 camellia bushes, and anyone would think . . ." At this point the audience is lost, many are asleep, and several have turned off their hearing aids. Keep their interest by keeping it brief.

Prayer requests often stimulate the saints to lengthy exposés of the foibles of the faithful:

I'm sure you'll all want to pray for Sister Sarah once again. She has surely had a string of sorrows weighing her down. This time, it's her teenage daughter who has fallen into sin and surely needs our prayers. This misfortune comes hard upon her husband's untimely death, God rest his soul, leaving her penniless and heartbroken with nothing to drive but the old Edsel. I hesitate to bring up the plight of her two sons, but the Lord is leading me to share their fall from grace so you can pray with wisdom. . . ."

Keep it brief, and never say publicly anything you couldn't say if Sister Sarah was standing in the sanctuary.

Make It Complimentary

Many chairmen tend to hide their own insecurities by shifting the blame for potential failure onto other people: "If only I had a decent committee, we might accomplish something"; "The district chairman never sent me so much as a postcard"; "When I was president, things were really organized, but now . . ."; "After what happened to this chairmanship last year, it will be a miracle if I can pull this thing together at all."

When I was president of our local women's club, the magazine chairman stood up to give her report. To win district acclamation she needed 100 percent of us to subscribe to the national journal, so she devised a way to achieve these results. She began by reading off a list of names and asking all those mentioned to stand up. Each lady when called upon stood up, smiled, and turned from side to side so all could see her. When the whole list had been read, the chairman asked everyone to look at them. In the midst of this mystery adulation, the chairman stated clearly, "These ladies you are looking at are the only ones in the club who have not renewed their subscriptions and are keeping this club from a district award."

The group of women standing sank instantly and gasped in unison. The ladies were insulted, and the whole club was indignant. The chairman got her 100 percent, but she was never nominated for any position again!

Don't make any negative remarks, even if you think they're cute. Keep your comments positive and complimentary.

From these narrations of the negatives, it is easy to conclude that if an announcement is worth making at all, it should be clear and to the point. It should be given with a bright, positive enthusiasm. It should be brief and include no chronicle of personal problems, and it should never insult another person, but be complimentary.

If each chairman could be coached to follow these instructions, every committee, club, or study would have such pleasant, positive people that everyone would want to join!

Today practice making a positive announcement at the dinner table.

ADDITIONAL CHALLENGES FOR MEN:

Women's clubs don't have a monopoly on boring business meetings. Many times men who have been too busy to prepare for a presentation ramble on in hope that a bright idea will land on their heads like a dove of peace. Whether in church or corporation or civic club, you can have a positive influence by setting an example. Few people have been trained to speak well, and if you have the opportunity to stand up front to announce or promote an activity, make it clear, positive, brief, and complimentary. Don't try to be funny by adding jokes or making sport of someone in the group. These antics make you look foolish and are usually received with a loud groan of disbelief. Remember: A leader has to be a step above others, not a rung below.

If you are in a position to train church leaders, for example, give them hypothetical events and let them stand up and practice giving an announcement on the subject. Let the people evaluate each other. All of the succeeding pages on introductions and presiding at meetings will give you additional material for practice. Men and women alike need to know how to give an announcement, how to introduce a friend or speaker, and how to preside properly over a meeting.

Why don't you call the meeting to order, begin to train others, and eliminate boredom from your board meetings?

Teach others to give an announcement.

It takes so little to be above average.

—CHAPTER TWENTY-THREE—

A Proper Introduction

Often one of the most pathetic platform presentations is the introduction of a guest speaker. I have been introduced with the reading of lengthy lists of everything I've ever done in my life or, at the other end of the scale, I've heard, "There is so much to say about Florence Littauer that I'm not going to say anything. So here she is." The long list puts them to sleep before the speaker gets up, and the "here she is" makes them wonder if there was, in fact, *anything* to say about her.

One night I was scheduled to speak at a mother-daughter banquet held in a long room about the size of two bowling alleys. On one side was a folding plastic wall, and on the far side of that was a strolling mariachi band in full swing. As the audience arrived, I discovered that few mothers had come—just little girls and their grandmothers. I looked around for the microphone and there was none. Realizing there was no way these elderly ladies could hear me over the band without a mike, I asked the chairman if I could stand halfway down the side of the room. When it was time for me to speak, the chairman announced, "Our speaker tonight does not want to stand here by the head table where a normal speaker would stand. She's down there somewhere in the middle of you all. Oh yes, there she is." She waved her hand toward me and sat down without having even given my name. I waited in amazement for the introduction, but she rose up slightly from her chair and called out, "Well, get on with it."

By this introduction she communicated clearly that I was not normal, I had strange ideas, I had been at least momentarily lost, my talk would be a chore to listen to, and my name was not significant enough to mention.

How much worse could she have done? Could she learn how to introduce a speaker? In CLASS we have a popular section on introductions, and so many people say they will never be afraid of this assignment again. In fact, we encourage our graduates to volunteer to introduce guests in their clubs or churches to spare the speaker an awkward start.

Oh, how we need people who can correctly introduce a speaker! Although professional speakers will usually have a prepared introduction which they request you read with enthusiasm, the average local speaker will rely on you to come up with something to say. What should you do?

Few people look upon the introduction with significance, and yet it serves a vital purpose. Picture the speaker sitting on the stage waiting to be introduced. We will assume Mrs. Stephens is unknown to the group. The ladies at the luncheon have already prejudged her. Those who assume they are arbiters of proper attire have decided she is not stylishly dressed and is probably too religious. The spiritual giants of the group have noticed the speaker is wearing eye makeup and therefore is probably not even a Christian. The intellectuals think she hasn't passed the seventh grade, and the insecure see her as intimidating because she carries a briefcase. These conflicting thoughts fill the air and build an invisible wall between the audience and the speaker, who may never be able to break it down.

The purpose of an introduction is to break down "the middle wall of partition between us" (Ephesians 2:14). These brief moments should be prepared carefully to achieve this desired result, to break down the wall between the speaker and the audience. Think of yourself as the connecting link between the two, as a bridge from the mouth of the speaker to the mind of the hearer. Your words can interest the audience in the speaker or turn them off. You have an awesome responsibility.

The preparation. You should present enough information to establish credentials, show why the speaker is gifted on his subject, and give the audience a reason to listen. Don't read an endless list of schools attended, and be sure you don't give away the plot of the message. Picture what it does to me when the introducer says, "Florence's wedding was in *Life* magazine, and later both her sons were born with brain damage."

There goes the fun and the trauma right out of my talk. Why not let the introducer give the whole speech, if he or she has already given away the heart of the message? Don't turn the introduction into a speech of your own, and don't get off the track. Don't wait until it's time to get up to begin interviewing the speaker with a "What's your name again, honey?"

The plan. In order to make an effective presentation, you should answer for the audience the following questions: Who? What? Where? and Why?

As an example, the audience needs to know the speaker's name—the *who* (and be sure you pronounce it properly); *what* talents, abilities, or credits he or she has that somewhat pertain to today's group; *where* he or she is from; and *why* this person was chosen to speak for this occasion.

Remember these four simple words: *who, what, where,* and *why* (the "Five Journalistic W's" without the *when*). The *when* is now. Using this outline can give you the ability to quickly interview anyone at any time and come up with an appropriate introduction. By adding the one word *when* to your format, you will have the formula for writing information for publicity, posters, newspaper articles, radio, and TV announcements.

The presentation. When it is time for the introduction, walk confidently to the podium. Try to do your part without notes, if possible, and keep your purpose in mind: break down that middle wall of partition between the speaker and audience. Be brief and enthusiastic. Be interesting and positive. Don't give away the plot. While most introducers are not engaging enough, a few go overboard in their praise of the speaker. Occasionally, I'll have some bubbly lady tell the audience that I'm a cross between Erma Bombeck and Phyllis Diller, and that I'll keep them in stitches. This oversell causes those who didn't want to be there in the first place to glare at me and send messages like, "You just try to make us laugh."

From here on you will enjoy evaluating those who introduce others, and you will learn from both their strengths and weaknesses. When someone asks, "Who will introduce the speaker?" please volunteer.

For those of you who are saying to yourselves right now, "If she thinks I'm getting up on a stage, she's crazy," let me point out how important it is to be able to introduce a person correctly in social situations. So many people are so insecure with introductions that they tend to ignore a new person or neglect a friend who is new to the group. Whether or not your neighbor wants to return next week to the Bible study may depend upon how well you introduce her this week: "This is my friend Sally. She works part-time as a nurse at the local hospital, and her hobby is raising African violets. She just moved here from Chicago. She came today to meet new people. I know you'll all enjoy getting acquainted with Sally."

People who once passed through Chicago, ever went to a hospital, or own a single African violet will have a basis for conversation because of your bright and brief introduction.

Memorize *who, what, where,* and *why,* and with these four words you'll be able to introduce anyone, anywhere, at any time.

Practice introducing your children at dinner this evening.

ADDITIONAL CHALLENGES FOR MEN:

Often men are ill at ease in social situations because they're not sure what to say or do. Mother either never told you how to introduce a person properly, or she made it so complicated that you never could remember how to do it. Do you present the older to the younger, or is it the other way around? To be secure, describe the new person to those who live locally.

Who: This lovely lady is my mother-in-law.
What: She just moved here from Chicago.
Where: She just flew in from Phoenix.
Why: She's come to visit us for the summer.

Remember that a pleasant smile and complimentary attitude is more important than protocol procedures (unless, of course, you are the director of protocol). A snobbish person who knows the rules can still be offensive. In these days of corporate downsizing, a man who is at ease with social skills will outlast the bumbler. Be the gracious gentleman and give a proper introduction.

It takes so little to be above average

CHAPTER TWENTY-FOUR

Preside Over
the Meeting

*B*ecause I have the popular Sanguine nature and love
to be up front, plus some traits of the Choleric, the
born leader, I have gone through many presidential
periods in my life. I once became president of the state speech
organization on my first meeting before I had even joined. It's
not hard to become president, because no one else wants the
responsibility. Those of us who know how to run a meeting
should volunteer in order to save the group from a year of
ineptitude and apathy. Are you ready to be a leader? It takes
so little to be above average.

Whenever pollsters survey Americans' fears, they always
find that "standing in front of a group" is number one on
their list. We are all so afraid of either being laughed at or
looking foolish in front of others that we prefer not to try at
all. Jim Newman, a fellow member of the National Speaker's
Association, in his book *Release Your Brakes* explains the
feelings people have when faced with even a supportive
audience:

When a person first joins Toastmasters, the pressure of standing in front of a few friendly, encouraging people can be pretty heavy. Some will find very creative reasons for not being able to come back and others will return and further develop their skills.

Those who return probably have no more potential, but they are responding to the pressure in a very different way. When you see an outstanding speaker performing with great enthusiasm and confidence, you can be sure that he has been subjected to the same pressures that have been felt by every other public speaker. He has not gritted his teeth and forced himself to continue. . . . Instead, he has formed the habit of responding to the successively higher levels of pressure in a positive way, using them as turn-ons instead of tie-ups.[1]

How about you? Do you have enough confidence in your ability to respond to leadership pressure in a positive way? Or could you if you had some guidelines on how to run a meeting?

What will you do when asked to be president of the social club or chairman of the Prudish Priscilla Circle? What about you men when a promotion in business requires chairing a few meetings? Will you, like Moses, say, "Who me? I am slow of tongue," or will you realize God has prepared you for such a time as this? So few men or women have any idea of how to run a meeting that you will appear brilliant if you say, "Will the opening meeting of the Choir Robe Committee (or the sales trainees) come to order." Take whatever opportunity presents itself and become a leader. Jump in where others fear to tread. It takes so little to be above average.

Purpose

Every group needs a leader, and we will assume that it is you! Begin by finding out what the purpose of your group is and what its chief function is to be. As you ask the past president, the pastor, and the people what the purpose is, you may be amused at the conflicting answers and instantly see why this group hasn't gone very far in the past.

So few leaders take the time or effort to find out what the purpose of the group is and bumble through half the year before finding out no one knows where they're going. If there is no true goal, either think one up or disband the group.

As soon as you have a goal in mind, try to state it in a simple and, if possible, catchy way and repeat it often to the group. They will feel so much more comfortable when they know why they are meeting, and repetition is essential. When I teach CLASS, on the first morning I review four major points: Problem, Purpose, Plan, and Personality. These are clearly written in the workbook, and each time I move on to a new one I review the previous ones. The fifth "P" is Practice, and when I get to this I mention it, but I don't make a point of this "P" being the conclusion of the list. The next morning I have the audience recite back the outline showing what they learned. They all recall the first four clearly, but when asked for the fifth, no one remembers what it was. Even though it was printed in the same type as the others and I mentioned it once, it does not stay in their minds because I didn't make the connection for them.

If you want anything remembered, state it, explain it, and repeat it. Start each meeting with the yearly purpose and the goal for that meeting. "This year we wish to double our membership, and our aim today is to plan the member-ship tea." "This year we must increase our sales by 20 percent, and your effort will make the difference."

Before you start your term in office, find a copy of the bylaws and read them. This step alone will make you above average as no one else even knows there are any (and possibly you didn't in the past).

You may find some original purposes that have long been ignored or some ideas that will make your yearly plan more vital.

When I was elected president of the Women's Club of San Bernardino, I read the bylaws and found one of our neglected goals was to foster spiritual values in our members. On this principle I had the grounds to start a Bible study in our clubhouse and initiate a prayer breakfast. For our efforts, we won a special state award for spiritual values and ethics and were instrumental in organizing district, state, and ulti-mately, national prayer breakfasts.

Know all you can about the background and bylaws of your organization, adopt a realistic goal for the year, and repeat your purpose or slogan often enough to make mem-bers remember it and to inspire them to achieve it.

Preparation

The big secret in confident leadership is being prepared. There is no way you can be consistent in conducting your meetings if you run in at the last minute and try to pull the thing together. We had a pastor once who often came to the Wednesday-night Bible study with no idea of what he was going to do. When he was prepared he would walk in briskly, go immediately to the pulpit, and present an exciting program.

On those nights when he would come in and casually shake hands with every person in an aisle seat, I knew he wasn't ready, and I prayed that the Holy Spirit would reveal a three-point outline to him as he wandered through the church.

Preparation is essential for your own self-confidence and for the comfort of other people. When you are agitated, they get nervous. In business, lack of preparation may mean the termination of your position.

How to prepare for a meeting—Take out a pad of paper and, for your own benefit, write the broad purpose of the club or business and the specific goal for the day across the top of your page. If you don't know what your goal is, it's more difficult to achieve it. This page will become your practice agenda. Start by listing all the regular items of business.

The Agenda

Call to order—"Will the October 15 meeting of the Women's Club of San Bernardino please come to order." In a more casual setting, "May I have your attention, please."

Thought for the day or opening prayer—To make your job easier, it is well to assign a responsible person who will give this opening thought. If the designated person forgets to come, it is the one who made the assignment who must fill in. Delegate every job possible so that your mind is free to conduct the meeting and have it all make sense. Even in business a motivational quote of the day will settle people down.

Pledge of Allegiance—If your group is not this formal, list whatever routine items must be handled in the beginning. This would include introductions of new staff or members.

Secretary's report—The best way to keep this report clear and concise and not a review of the secretary's recent vacation to Hawaii is to make it a policy right from the beginning that she write her report within 24 hours of the meeting and get a copy in your hands within three days. This practice increases the chances for accuracy and gives you time to correct errors and cross out trivia. After you have updated her report, return it with a note of praise for how few things you had to add or delete. This plaudit will make her want to do better next time and keep her from resenting your corrections.

At the end of her reading the report ask: "Are there any errors or omissions?" If there are not any say, "The report is approved as read." If there are changes, accept them, and then say, "The report is approved as corrected." If you also have a correspondence secretary, have her read any notes or letters at this point.

Treasurer's report—Since most women get nervous at the mention of a budget, you should insist that this report be as brief as possible. I always made sure I knew what the figures were about, and then I could give a review in layman's language of what the treasurer had said. Sometimes the report is just to read for information, but other groups want a chance to discuss the finances. Conclude with, "The treasurer's report is approved as read" or "The treasurer's report is approved as corrected."

Some organizations print up the treasurer's report, pass it out to all, and don't read it in the meeting, assuming no one really cares.

Old business—Whatever is pending from the last meeting should be dealt with first, so list these items. The best way to know you won't forget something is to read over your collection of minutes from the last few meetings. I would always review the minutes from the same month the previous year to spot some matter that should be brought up every October or every January.

After each item is announced and discussed, the presiding officer is to ask for a motion on the subject. It is best if you state a possible motion that is clear and will allow for either a yes or no response and then have a member restate the motion. It is never the chairman's prerogative to give personal opinions which will sway the group. When a motion is made, ask for a second to that motion. Then repeat the motion as stated, say it has been made and seconded, and instruct, "All those in favor, please say aye. All opposed, please say no." There is no reason to take a count unless the vote is in question. Then say, "The ayes have it, and we have just voted to . . ."

New business—The procedure will be the same as old business except that many of these items may be suggested by other members. My policy was to have the suggestion or motion in writing ahead of the meeting or it would not be discussed. Members actually like the meetings better when they are brief and purposeful. Your attendance will rise or fall according to the interest or the boredom of your meetings.

AGENDA

Date:_____

Names ·

Purpose:

Call to order

Thought or prayer

Pledge of Allegiance

Secretary's report

Correspondence secretary's report

Treasurer's report

Old business

New business

Committee reports

Miscellaneous items

Adjournment

Program introduction

Closing remarks and/or prayer

The sample agenda on page 208 is to give you an idea of how to prepare for a meeting that will be done "decently and in order." Some of you will strip this down to meet the simplicity of your small committee, and a few of you may want to expand it. If you wish to have a deeper understanding of parliamentary procedure, study *Robert's Rules of Order,* the Bible of leadership.

Committee reports—In order to keep chairmen working, you must allow them to report their progress and commend them for whatever step forward they may have made. As with new business, I always asked the chairmen to let me know before the meeting if they intended to give a report so that I could place them on the agenda. No notice, no report.

Miscellaneous items—Your group may have some specialized items or announcements that must be made at this point. Discourage personal pet projects that can drag the meeting down.

At this point thank everyone who has done anything remotely significant. Since most people thrive on praise and plaudits, please give them. Consistent compliments and credit will place you way above average.

Adjournment—Ask for any last-minute items of business and then say, "I declare the meeting of the (name of organization) to be adjourned." If you are conducting a corporate meeting that does not need to be officially adjourned, give a concluding summary of what has been accomplished and review the goals for the future. Don't just say, "Well, I guess that's it for today."

Program—If there is to be a program, adjourn the formal meeting and then call upon the program chairman to introduce the speaker. Your job should be over unless a wrap-up or benediction is needed at the end.

Now that you have written the practice agenda and have filled in all the business items, set the paper aside for a few days. As ideas or phone calls come in, add to the page. The day before the meeting, reread, correct, and type the final agenda. When I had my finished copy in hand, I would then underline the major items with colored pens so that I could pick them out at a glance. In the margin I would add the name of the person who was doing the prayer, the secretary, the report chairman, etc., in big print next to the corresponding item. I never assumed I would remember even my best friend's name when up front, so I listed everyone and highlighted the names. I could see the names easily and therefore never stumbled over one or wondered who was next.

When you know your agenda is complete, run off some copies for the secretary, the vice president, the parliamentarian, and any other people who need to have an itemized list of the day's proceedings. At the first meeting when you walk in with a neat agenda in triplicate, the word will spread quickly that you mean business and that they have a president who is above average.

In your preparation to lead your group, if you don't have an office, it is essential that you have someplace in your home that is just for this group's materials. If you don't have a desk, try a drawer, briefcase, or at least a box. The minute anything comes in for this organization, put it in the proper place. If you let papers drift around the house waiting for a day to sort them out, you may never see them again. I had one secretary in a women's club who left her minutes on the kitchen counter. When she went to find them, they were gone and she arrived without a report. At the next meeting she told us her son had picked them up by mistake, had stapled them into the middle of his college term paper, and they had received a B+.

Even if you have a correspondence secretary, you should go through the mail. She may not know what you consider important or how you want a note answered. At a time-management seminar I learned to handle each piece of mail only once. As you read the letter for the first time, underline what needs attention and write the name of who should take action on this item. Before each meeting hand out the mail to those who should follow through, and hope for the best. If it's crucial, double-check to see that it's been done.

Presentation

On the day when you are to preside (or introduce the speaker or give an announcement), arrive early with your wisdom and wits about you. Pass out your agendas to those who need a copy and open the meeting on time. Remember, you set the tone on clothing, manners, and punctuality. If there is a microphone, use it since there are often people who are hard of hearing.

Many women are terrified of anything mechanical and pull back while expressing, "I have a loud voice. I don't need a mike." I have learned that women who are boisterous and even garrulous offstage oftentimes act just the opposite when giving the flea market report. I ignore their "loud voice" comments and, with a firm hand on the shoulder, ease them into the mike. To give others courage to speak up, you must be confident in using the equipment yourself, even if you must come an hour early to practice.

In the 30 years I have been involved with all types of club, church, and organizational work, I have found that when the presiding officer leads with loving authority, the group will follow with respect. But if this person is insecure, nervous, and confused, the crowd may swoop in as vultures. If you know the purpose of your position, have a clear goal for the year, have done your homework, arrive early and prepared, you will preside with confidence.

Today think of what organization could benefit from your leadership ability.

ADDITIONAL CHALLENGES FOR MEN:

Unfortunately, the superior male business image doesn't automatically mean that men are genetically equipped to run meetings better than women. In fact, some of the worst meetings I've attended have been chaired by men who hadn't done their homework or who somehow weren't listening to their own agenda. Perhaps the poorest of all was the Sunday school teachers' meeting chaired by the pastor, who obviously had better things to do—as we all did. One young man who taught the junior high class spent much time explaining why his group of students no longer wished to go to opening exercises: 1. Mrs. Armey was too old and they made fun of her. 2. These preteens were too sophisticated to have to sit with the little kids. 3. He worked hard preparing his lesson and needed more time to teach it. His proposal met with more discussion than I could have imagined. Would this set a precedent? Would the fourth and fifth grades want to quit opening exercises also? Would Mrs. Armey be upset? Would the parents care one way or another? Finally, we took a vote and decided to let this young man keep his group for the whole hour so he could teach them even more. This vote was not unanimous and left Mrs. Armey's best friend quite upset.

As we all calmed down, this same young man stated that he had a second item of business. He was going to quit teaching his class so he could devote more time to the bus ministry. He was going to quit after getting an extension on his teaching time? I was in a state of shock as I heard the pastor ask how many were in favor of accepting the man's resignation. There was a murmur of approval, and we then moved on. No one mentioned the inconsistency of these two requests, and I didn't stay around long enough to find out if the next teacher wanted extra time or would have been thrilled to sit and listen to Mrs. Armey each Sunday.

I'm sure that you men who care enough to read this book are above average and would have done a better job, but the pastor, a well-educated man, is still at that same church with the same people running the same meetings.

Let's be prepared, do our homework, and pay attention to what's going on. Why not volunteer to be in charge? No one else really wants the job!

Preside over the meetings.

It takes so little to be above average.

PART VI

It Takes So Little to Entertain Above Average

— CHAPTER TWENTY-FIVE —

Be a Lover
of Hospitality

*[Be] a lover of hospitality, a lover of
good men, sober, just, holy, temperate.*
—Titus 1:8

I have always been a "lover of hospitality." I've had
parties for any possible reason and celebrated every
holiday known to man. Over the years I've collected
decorations and centerpieces for every season and have
known where they were for display at the right time. As my
children grew up, they became lovers of hospitality, also. We
have had extra people living with us off and on for over 40
years, and entertaining strangers has been a way of life.

After our family all dedicated their lives to the Lord, He
moved us from our comfortable social position in Connecticut,
where our house was used for the "opening teas" of everything,
to "Bungalow One" in California. Looking back on it, the Lord
really had a sense of humor to take a person who had spent her
life working up to the big home and the country club, then
plunk her into a dilapidated, abandoned bungalow. Hadn't He
promised me an abundant, not abandoned, life? Why was I
sentenced to hard labor in a shell of a motel? When we had
been asked to go on staff with Campus Crusade for Christ, I

somehow pictured Fred and me on a spiritual cloud floating through life with the greats of the faith while a choir sang majestically in the background. How quickly I fell off the cloud when I found I was to live in Bungalow One—five motel rooms, each with a door opening onto a patio. There wasn't even a kitchen, so I had to cook for my family on a hot plate on a porch. How could anyone be a lover of hospitality in such a setting?

Oh, what a lesson the Lord had in mind for me! He had to teach me that it wasn't the surroundings but the spirit that made for genuine hospitality. As a family, we crowded into those five little rooms and, to put us to a further test, the Lord sent "strangers" to live with us. We had four girls layered in one room, and when my mother came to visit, we added a third bunk bed on the top of two others. Each night Marita lay with her head inches from the ceiling. Young Fred and nephew Dwayne were in bunks in the next room, and Fred and I had a motel room at the far end.

We made the porch into a kitchen, and we ate a few feet from the sink. The table filled all the available space, and whoever sat in the back couldn't get out short of a fire. There was no place to shelve all my assorted sets of dishes, and my centerpieces were retired to storage in "Bungalow Two." I had come full circle. After the great climb to success, I was back in "three rooms behind the store."

Could I ever entertain in Bungalow One? With eight around a crowded table every night, could we add even one more? Psalm 101:6 (TLB) says, "I will make the godly of the land my heroes, and invite them to my home." Surely, the godly of the land passed through Arrowhead Springs, and I found what they wanted most was a home-cooked meal in a friendly atmosphere. Since Fred and I spend so much of our time traveling to and eating in motels, I can now understand how they enjoyed our home life. I can see why the spirit of togetherness was more important than the space.

I became the "Martha of the Hill," cooking and serving the godly of the Lord. Dr. Henry Brandt sat at our table many nights, and I learned from him the skills of counseling. So much of what I do automatically today came from the hours of advice I received from Dr. Brandt. Howard Blandau helped Lauren adjust to this unexpected move in her early teen years, and evangelist Ernie Wilson held my little 5-year-old Fred in his arms on each visit. Eleanor Whitney taught me much about Christian speaking, and Barbara Fain schooled me as a Bible-study teacher. Ian Thomas enthralled us with his English accent, and Hal Lindsey introduced us to prophecy. Christian speakers and leaders from all over the world crowded into Bungalow One and filled our family reservoirs with rich experiences. My children now refer to this time as mother's Hostess on the Hill era.

Could I ever entertain in Bungalow One? Oh, yes. I could and did. Hospitality doesn't depend on size, but on spirit. In fact, the dictionary says hospitality is "the spirit of being hospitable," which is "behaving in a kind and generous manner toward guests, fond of entertaining."[1]

While I was living in Bungalow One, I was asked to give the Campus Crusade staff instructions on "courtesy and manners" and also to teach a Christian living course at a local church. During my time of preparation for these two classes, I interviewed over 200 people on their experiences and attitudes on entertaining. I started with the assumption that everyone did entertain, devising a chart for people to check off: How often do you have company? How many people do you invite? For what kind of an occasion? Much to my surprise, I found that few had anybody in for any reason. These results shifted my emphasis from *how* to entertain to *why*.

Why should Christians entertain? The Bible tells us to "use hospitality one to another without grudging" (1 Peter 4:9). Peter tells us to open up our homes without complaining. How often I hear a woman bemoaning the fact that she has to have some people over. How much fun will these guests have? How do I feel when a lady tells me she can't come to my seminar because she's been assigned to cook my dinner and it will take her all day. As she sighs, I wonder if I'm worth eight hours of preparation. Wouldn't it be better if she came to the sessions? We would then have a mutual subject for conversation while letting the "Colonel" do the cooking.

> *Be not forgetful to entertain strangers: for thereby some have entertained angels unawares* (Hebrews 13:2).

In our two years in Bungalow One and in the following years, we have entertained many strangers who turned out to be angels. I remember one time bringing home a visiting missionary nurse who was on leave from Zaire. None of us knew much about Zaire and, up until then, had not cared to. One family policy we have adopted is to always ask the guest to explain what it is he or she does. Frequently, these people are shy and will not push into the conversation of a verbose family. Fred encourages them to share, and we then can get the benefits we might have missed.

Young Fred, ten years old at the time, brought out his globe so the nurse could show him where Zaire was. She held him spellbound as she explained a culture to him he had never known existed. That night when she showed slides at church, he was in the front row.

What a wonderful benefit it can be to entertain strangers! But remember to encourage them into sharing, or you will miss the blessing.

> *Distributing to the necessity of saints; given to hospitality* (Romans 12:13).

The Bible says we should open our homes to strangers. Feeding groups at a moment's notice is not easy, but as you get in the habit, it can be fun. I always made sure to have staples on hand for certain basic dishes, and when Fred let me know at five o'clock that a few friends were in town, I was able to put together an adequate meal. No one expects a gourmet treat; they just enjoy a simple meal at home.

As I was raising my children, they always got excited about having company "overnight," whether it was their friends or strangers. They all knew they could bring home anyone who needed a place to stay, and we have thereby entertained many "angels unawares."

In 1 Timothy 3:2 we learn that a Christian leader was to be "given to hospitality," and in chapter 5, verse 10, that a godly woman must have "lodged strangers" and "washed the saint's feet."

Why should Christians entertain? Because the Bible tells us so.

Today discuss with your family their ideas of hospitality.

ADDITIONAL CHALLENGES FOR MEN:

Once you understand the scriptural admonition to entertain strangers and angels, you will want to encourage your wife to invite people in for simple sharing in your home. If you are the Sanguine, the party lover, you enjoy an audience for your humor, but your wife may need everything to be perfect before she lets anyone in the front door. Let her know you will help in the preparation and cleanup, and then be sure to follow through.

If you are the Choleric take-charge person, you tend to invite those people who can benefit you somewhere down the line. Force yourself to invite some people who appear to have nothing to offer you. You might find an occasional angel unawares.

If you are the perfectionist Melancholy, you may have a casual, fun-loving wife, who never has the house in the right order to suit you. If you do have company, you tend to apologize for your wife's mistakes, making your wife and the guests very nervous. Relax! Remember, it's not the dust but the delight of the moment that matters.

If you are the peaceful Phlegmatic, your wife considers you lazy, and she knows you won't lift a finger to help her. Surprise her! Get off the couch and move—in any direction. One lady told me that when she got married, her husband and the couch became one.

Ask her what you can do, and then do it. Your friends already like you; now help your wife to love you. Look at your differing personalities and discuss how much and what kind of entertaining you will do. There's nothing worse than visiting a home where the host couple is bickering and contentious.

Encourage your wife to entertain, and then help her to do it without complaint.

Be a lover of your wife and of hospitality.

It takes so little to be above average.

CHAPTER TWENTY-SIX

Entertain Strangers and Saints

I f we know we should be lovers of hospitality, *why don't we entertain more often?* The following are actual excuses I've been given. Have you ever used one of these?

My house is too small. How big was Bungalow One? When one lady told me she had never had me over because her house was too small, I asked, "How big do you think I am? I only need one average-size chair." She thought it over for a minute and replied, "I guess I've been using that as an excuse for years. I figured if you didn't have a big house, you didn't have to have company."

My house isn't decorated yet. I have one friend who told me for ten years she would have me over when she got the house done. Once I arrived unexpectedly to deliver something to her, and she kept me out on the front step because the house wasn't ready. I really expected someday that the great unveiling would come, but she moved away before that happened.

I don't have good china. Who cares? I happen to love all kinds of beautiful china, but if you'll feed me, I sure won't care if the dishes even match. If this problem is not just an excuse, watch for bargains. Having place settings of odd patterns is in vogue at the moment.

I'm not a good cook. Now there's a real excuse . . . or is it? One Sunday in the calendar section of the *Los Angeles Times* I counted 40 different cooking classes in the area. Recipes abound in every women's magazine, and there is the *Too Busy to Cook* cookbook that guarantees a gourmet meal in 30 minutes. One evening I was served an excellent creamed chicken on flaky pastry shells and, when I complimented the hostess, she said, "I'm really not a good cook, but I don't let that keep me from entertaining. I bought a few pouches of Stouffer's Creamed Chicken and heated up the frozen shells. Most people seem to like it." So did I.

I'm too disorganized. If you don't know how to organize your household, read a book like *More Hours in My Day* by Emilie Barnes. Emilie has also written *The Spirit of Loveliness* (how to do everything with the right spirit) and *If Teacups Could Talk* (giving recipes and decorative ideas for tea-party entertaining). I've known Emilie for 25 years, and she doesn't teach anything that she hasn't already lived herself. If you don't have time to read a book today but you have to entertain tomorrow, I'll give you a simple plan in the next chapter.

My mother never entertained. Having been brought up eating in the variety store with customers watching, I was surely never steeped in the social graces. In college I took out books on etiquette and watched the housemother serve. I'm still reading and learning from others. You may have a positive heritage from your mother, but if she didn't ever entertain, don't use that as an excuse. Be creative on your own.

I don't have enough money. If this is a valid excuse, you might consider having people over for coffee after church or hosting an occasional potluck supper. People don't mind bringing something to eat if you'll do the setup and cleanup. *I don't know whom to ask.* I find people to ask on every corner. Fred and I have always made it a custom to look around for new faces in church and invite them home for Sunday brunch. We have met new friends this way, and many have said they kept coming to the church because we were friendly. When I was president of the women's club, I got a list of all the ladies who were going to be alone for Christmas. I passed around a sign-up sheet for those members who would like to have them into their homes. When I received the papers back, I was stunned to find no one put her name on the list. When I asked around, the answer was, "Christmas is a personal holiday, and we don't want any outsiders around." We always had outsiders around, and we entertained many angels unawares.

We don't like the same people. This is often just an excuse, but sometimes it is a problem. The wife has all Christian friends and the husband's friends "might swear." One man told me, "All her friends are so saintly that it makes me sick!" It is important that we don't turn each dinner party into a tent meeting that turns off nonbelievers. Have your Bible studies in the daytime and your evangelistic girlfriends for lunch, and aim for dinner guests with whom your husband can feel comfortable.

Fred and I have been victims of evenings when at dessert the hostess would say, "Now you two give your testimony," hoping we would save her husband over apple pie. We went to a party one night where the lady had promised her husband she wouldn't do anything religious. However, she had invited a young man to give an evangelistic talk and end with an invitation prayer. As the surprise guest spoke, her husband shifted in his seat and was obviously upset at this sneaky program. To make him think it wasn't really religious, she jumped in right after the "Amen" and said "Let's all sing a chorus or two of 'There's a Shanty in Old Shanty Town.'" Somewhat aghast, we all weakly sang about the shanties as her husband disappeared from view. Not all saints and sinners are socially compatible, but it is possible to win the world with a loving spirit without ever quoting a verse. Let them see you care for them, and they will want to know why.

People don't come on time. Isn't that the truth! But don't expect them to come on time. If I want to serve dinner at 7:00 P.M., I have them come at 6:30 and have some snacks and punch available. I make sure I don't have many last-minute things to do, and I never put the rolls in until the roll's been called.

People don't leave on time. They must be having a good time! If this is a genuine problem, state on the invitation 7–9 P.M. or say on the phone, "We have to be up early the next day, so we'll be finishing up about nine." We once had some people who just wouldn't leave, so Fred finally stood up and said, "I hope you'll excuse me, but I must get to bed." This is not the most gracious thing to do, but in desperation it will work.

People don't ask us back. Join the club! In my social days I used to keep a record of which people had us over so I could keep even. Once a good friend told me, "I'm not inviting you over Sunday night because when I checked I didn't owe you a dinner." As I began to study Christian hospitality, I found in Luke 14:12-14 (TLB), "When you put on a dinner . . . don't invite friends, brothers, relatives, and rich neighbors! For they will return the invitation. Instead, invite the poor, the crippled, the lame, and the blind. Then at the resurrection of the godly, God will reward you for inviting those who can't repay you." From these verses I learned that I was to be a lover of hospitality without ever expecting anything in return. While in Bungalow One almost all the people I entertained were those passing through town. I knew they would never invite me to their homes, but I gained much from the fellowship of the saints.

If these are only excuses, then what are the underlying reasons why we don't entertain?

> *Worry*—"I'm just sick for days before I have anyone over."
> *Fear of Failure*—"What if it doesn't turn out right?"
> *Pride*—"If I can't do it perfectly, I'm not going to do it at all."
> *Bitterness*—"No one ever has us over, and I'll just show them."
> *Selfishness*—"We're all so busy that when we have a spare minute, we just want to be alone."
> *Laziness*—"It's so much easier to stop by McDonald's."

As we agree that the Bible instructs us to entertain and we see the excuses or reasons why we don't, we can conclude that in the field of Christian hospitality, *it takes so little to be above average.*

Today show hospitality by inviting a new church member to brunch.

ADDITIONAL CHALLENGES FOR MEN:

According to your personalities, you and your wife probably see things from a different perspective. One of you wants fun, the other perfection. Or one of you wants to bring people in, and the other says it's just too much work. Sit down with your wife and discuss your differences. How often would you like to entertain? What kind of hospitality do you wish to extend?

Go over the list of excuses and see which ones are valid in your household. Determine to cooperate, do the best you can, and then relax.

A nervous host produces nervous guests.

Entertain strangers and saints.

It takes so little to be above average.

—CHAPTER TWENTY-SEVEN—

Prepare a Table

*A*ccording to Proverbs 31, the virtuous woman got up before dawn to prepare breakfast, and she bought food imported from afar. She also spent time each morning giving her servant girls instructions, and right there most of us lose contact with her. If we entertain, we have to do all the work. It seems overwhelming.

How can we make entertaining fun? First decide what type of entertaining you want to do. If you're inexperienced or unsure of yourself, don't start with an elegant dinner party for 12. What are different possibilities?

Simple Entertaining

Instead of the *sit-down dinner* where you may feel like a glorified waitress, you could try a *buffet supper* where the food is prepared, laid out on a buffet table, and guests serve themselves. They can sit at one table, several small tables, or on any available chair or couch.

The *potluck*, or covered-dish supper, can be set up the same as the buffet, but the guests bring at least part of the food. For several years when we lived in a large home, Fred and I had a potluck once a month on Saturday for any friends, plus their friends, who wanted to come. We did not assign specific items, and it usually came out about right. We set up tables all over the house, and I made matching table-cloths and napkins from sheets. I provided the house, prepared the tables, made coffee and tea, and cleaned up afterward. Each time we had some kind of entertainment or program. If a singing group was in town or a traveling speak-er, we would invite them to share. One February we prepared all kinds of material for making valentines and gave prizes for the most creative. We averaged about 50 people, and some-times had up to 90. It took above-average effort, but many people still remember the evenings of fun and fellowship.

Barbecues make entertaining simple—especially if your husband likes to cook. When weather permits, set up a pic-nic table, have hamburgers and rolls, an assortment of rel-ishes, and perhaps a salad. Men seem to be most relaxed when standing over the flames of a charcoal grill.

I like to have company for *brunch* because Fred makes crepes. After church I set the table while he prepares the bat-ter and makes coffee. By the time the guests arrive, we're ready to go. All we need on the table is butter and syrup, although often we add fruit and sour cream. People love to watch Fred cook, and he keeps at it as long as anyone will eat. The fellowship after church is relaxed and unpressured, and no one expects a big meal.

Theme parties, birthdays, or showers. Because we are a cre-ative family, we love to come up with different kinds of par-ties that have a theme. We've even celebrated Ground Hog

Day. For our twenty-fifth anniversary, Marita and Lauren gave us a surprise party. We had just moved from our big house to a condominium with strawberry-covered wallpaper in the kitchen. The girls sent invitations on strawberry note cards, and everyone was instructed to bring a strawberry gift wrapped in strawberry paper. For refreshments they served strawberry punch and bowls of huge strawberries.

For Fred's fiftieth birthday we had a 1950s party, and everyone was to wear what they would have been wearing in the fifties. I wore my honeymoon going-away suit of bright-red poodle cloth, and Marita was adorable in baby clothes with a ruffled bonnet. We had fifties music and relived our youth.

When Marita's book *Shades of Beauty* was published in July 1982, we wanted to give her a "success" party. Lauren hosted the party, tied rainbow ribbons to each rosebush that lined the entry to her house, and put a huge rainbow over the front door. She sent rainbow card invitations, had rainbow napkins, and a large rainbow arched across the cake. Lauren lined up pictures of Marita in her various life stages across the wall, and everyone shared what part they had played in Marita's climb to success.

With a little thought and planning any party can be above average.

Coffees and teas are about the simplest type of entertaining you can do (and often the most fun for all because you are relaxed). In these hurried days where few entertain formally, an invitation for coffee is welcomed. If you have some cookies or cheese and crackers, bring those out, but a sociable hour around a cup of coffee or tea can be a blessed time of sharing.

Let's assume you've chosen to have a simple dinner party and want it to go smoothly. What are some guidelines you can follow?

Dinner Party Entertaining

Plan

1. Make out a simple menu using dishes you know how to prepare. (Don't choose this event to try your first soufflé.)

2. Make a list of every ingredient you need to buy, and check those you think you have. Finding out at the last minute that your children have eaten a vital ingredient can ruin your evening.

3. Make a list of everything that has to be done. As your children grow up, you can assign them duties. I always made up a list of the items to be served, what platter or dish they were to go on, and who was responsible for putting it on the table. For example:

Meat and potatoes—wooden trencher—Florence
Tossed salad—black bowl with silver base—Lauren
Bread (heated)—straw basket—Marita
Butter—crystal butter dish—Fred, Jr.
Water (fill glasses)—silver pitcher—Fred, Sr.

We all had our duties and handled them at the right time.

4. Check off the list as you go along. This prevents you from forgetting the rolls until they're burned black or finishing the whole meal with the relish tray still in the refrigerator.

Prepare

1. Do the marketing a day ahead. On times when I haven't followed my own advice, I've been running from

store to store at the last minute to find ladyfingers for the belated chocolate mousse that has to set three hours.

2. Prepare everything as early as possible. Never assume you will have a lot of time in the afternoon. Each one of us could write pages about emergencies that have ruined the best-laid plans.

3. Set the table early in the day. I've often done it the night before. Seeing that table set is a tranquilizer for you as you race around, and it's soothing to the guests also when they see you are indeed prepared.

4. Try to clean up the kitchen before the guests arrive. There is nothing more unnerving to the guests than to drift into your kitchen and find open cans sitting around, cooking dishes piled high in the sink, and batter dribbling into the open silverware drawer. Conversely, I've been complimented by guests who have commented, "I would never know you'd cooked a meal here."

5. Allow plenty of time to dress. I still have trouble realizing how long it takes to get dressed, even though I've been late many times. I now give myself twice what I think it will take, and I come out about even.

Present

1. Present yourself attractively at the door. I've been met at people's doors by all kinds of visions: rollers in the hair, nightgowns, bathing suits. What's worse is when no one comes or some little, unknown child opens the door. One evening Fred and I stood in a foyer trying to converse with a four-year-old and hoping we were in the right house.

2. Greet your guests warmly. Tell them how glad you are they could come. Don't let them sense tension or fear to

make them ill at ease. If you have to go right back to the kitchen, either seat them with your husband or a child or ask if they would like to join you while you finish the preparation. The tone of their first few minutes in your home gives them a mind-set for the evening.

3. Be natural, not trying to impress. There is nothing that unnerves guests so quickly as your trying to impress them with your great works. I've been in situations where the dear lady chronicled her whole week of preparing this dinner until I felt guilty I'd come. Be yourself. No one likes a phony, so relax. Even if something fails, it won't ruin your life or theirs.

4. Don't keep apologizing: "I got started so late today, I'll never get this on the table"; "I bet this is too sweet for you"; "This is a new recipe and I'm scared to death that it won't be right"; "I'm such a bad cook I don't know why I invited you." I've had all these said to me, some by the same lady in the same night. I would like the hostess to do her best and not hover over me in a sea of worry. Constant apologies make everyone nervous.

5. Don't point out your mistakes. We might not even notice, and knowing might ruin the meal. "I ran out of sugar so I used blackstrap molasses"; "After I mixed this all up I said to myself, 'This looks just like dog food'"; "This cake wasn't supposed to be an upside-down cake, but it sure is now. I dropped it on the floor, but I brushed it off, and I vacuumed yesterday anyway"; "I burned the carrots, so pretend they're caramelized." None of these errors, pointed out to guests, adds to one's appetite. As Julia Child says, "What they don't know won't hurt them." If you don't point out your mistakes, few people will ever notice them. But too graphic an explanation may kill their appetite.

Participate

1. Don't spend all your time in the kitchen. Guests would much rather have a simple meal with you at the table than something so complex you rarely show up. Fred and I had dinner one time where the hostess didn't even set herself a place. She explained, "I really want my guests to have a good time, so I do all I can to make them happy." She meant well, but we all felt uncomfortable as she ferried courses in and out of the kitchen by herself. When guests come to your home, they want to visit, so plan something that you can handle easily. How can we relax when you're so overworked?

2. Ask people to help you. It is not a sign of weakness to ask someone to assist you. I plan ahead what small jobs others can do. I find guests feel better doing something than sitting alone in the living room. Guests can take snacks or hors d'oeuvres to each other; they can man the punch bowl or pass out napkins. They can take a head count on coffee or tea and serve the dessert while you rinse the dishes. Always remember: Your aim is to treat the guests to a relaxing evening, not impress them with how hard you've worked just for them.

3. Have your husband participate. If your husband is willing, include him in your plans. Have him answer the door and take coats, get a beverage for the guests, keep them happy in the living room. Don't let him think this is your thing and he's too inept to help. I can always tell how a man is treated at home by how he reacts when I ask him to help me. If I ask a man to carry the punch bowl to the patio and he says, "Me? You want me to carry this glass bowl? You trust me?" I know he feels like a dummy at home. For some reason he's not a

contributing part of the family. Make your husband feel an important part of the festivities.

4. Have something for children to do. If you are still in the era when little ones arrive, it is well to plan ahead of time what to do with them. I often seated them at a separate table and had little favors or gifts to keep them happy. I usually fed them first so they could play in another room while we ate. Once when we had a big holiday party and I wanted our dinner to be special with no distractions, I hired a young girl across the street to come for two hours. Lauren made up sandwiches, chips, and cupcakes and put a little lunch for each child in separate bags. Just before the adults sat down to eat, we summoned the children and Lauren told them how much fun they were going to have on their picnic. They weren't to open their bags until they got to the picnic table we had set up in a vacant lot nearby. The sitter led them off so excited, and all of us had a pleasant meal.

5. Have a Plan B in mind if conversation fails. There are times when all the guests are brilliant and you wouldn't interrupt the flow for anything, but there are those evenings when nothing seems to click. What do you do? Fred and I have several Plan B's. We have had times when a quiet group came alive with some structured conversation. "Since many of you don't know each other, let's go around the table and introduce ourselves. Tell where you grew up, what schools you went to, what interests you have that are unusual, and what you'd do if you had all next week off with no responsibility." Always start with yourself, since what you say will set the tone. If you share for five minutes, they will, too. If you say it all in one sentence, that's all they will do.

One Mother's Day we had all the guests tell what they remembered about their mothers in their childhood. We had tender and touching stories exchanged. One Christmas we had each person tell what had been the most significant event in the past year. On Valentine's Day we asked about our childhood sweethearts and what became of them. Several times we've asked what goals people have in their personal growth and how they can achieve them. Other guests begin to give suggestions. It's amazing how people will respond when you first lead with a question of interest and then give the first example yourself.

So many people have something fascinating to say, but they don't think anyone cares to hear it. You be the one to coordinate the conversation, keeping it as even as possible so one person doesn't monopolize the night.

If you are a lover of hospitality, desiring to entertain strangers and saints and willing to prepare a table for others, you will delight the Lord and your guests.

Today set your dinner table for those special people: your family.

ADDITIONAL CHALLENGES FOR MEN:

Since you are 50 percent of this home-management team, you must be willing to participate in entertaining the saints. In this chapter I have given suggestions on simple and more formal entertaining. You and your wife need to determine together what is appropriate for you according to your finances, ability, and personalities. Because of personality differences, couples can't understand why one wants to have fun and the other considers company to be an imposition. Discuss your attitudes ahead of the invitation so that you can compromise and come to an agreement.

Many times businessmen expect their wives to entertain

customers lavishly, have everything prepared on time, and look like Martha Stewart when everyone arrives. Very few women today have the time or talent to produce a serene sit-down dinner for 12. If you wish this type of meal, take the afternoon off and help her (or take them all out to dinner and save your marriage).

Don't push your wife into feeding the boss if she is ill at ease in the kitchen. I've known women with brilliant minds who have never learned to do much more than microwave TV dinners, and I've seen many men who couldn't boil water. Don't put each other to the test and then complain about the results. Don't expect your wife to be your mother. They grew up in different eras with different backgrounds, experience, and personalities. Don't ever ridicule your wife in front of company and point out how poorly she's done. I have often been the victim of a dinner party where the husband continuously makes derogatory statements about his wife's culinary deficiencies. "I hope you're not starving because she's running way behind, as usual." "She always forgets the napkins." "The potatoes are lumpy again." "Can't you do anything right?" By the time the guests hear all this, they've lost their appetites and feel extreme compassion for the wife.

Remember, if you criticize your wife and point out her failures, assuming people will praise you for putting up with such an incompetent individual for so long, realize that's not how it goes. Instead, they feel sorry for her whether or not she is competent and wonder how she has put up with you for all these years.

Criticism comes back to haunt the one who gives it, while wiping out any hope in the one who receives it.

If mistakes are made, help her to cover them. Be her helpmate. She will be so grateful when you function with her and not against her that she might even invite your mother to bring her friends over for tea!

Help your wife to prepare a table.

It takes so little to be above average.

PART VII

It Takes So Little to Care Above Average

CHAPTER TWENTY-EIGHT

Relieve the Afflicted

S o far we have looked at areas which will make us all more confident and capable in thinking creatively, leading effectively, and entertaining without worry. Now that we have our own lives under control, it is time to think about others.

How does the average Christian treat the person with problems? How do we love the unlovable, the undesirable, the unpopular? What do we do with the ugly and the odd? How do we handle death, divorce, and despair?

Although originally I did not plan to cover such questions in this book, these thoughts kept coming to my mind. One day I presented this problem to the Lord and said, "If You want me to deal with these difficult dilemmas, show me." The next day I boarded a plane and sat in my customary bulkhead window seat. The aisle seat was taken and the middle seat empty. At the last minute a handsome young man, obviously distressed, plunked down next to me and said, "I'll never fly this airline again!" Since the Lord consistently sends me fascinating "plane partners," I inquired about his problem. After relating his annoyance, he calmed down and we began to discuss our lives and careers. I told him I was writing a book on how to be above average. He asked how I chose writing as a career, and I then gave him my testimony. When I got to the part about my two brain-damaged sons, I saw his expression change.

"I have a little girl with Apert's Syndrome," he whispered. "Perhaps you'll understand what we've been through." He told me how little Jennifer had been born with cranioserosis, a fusion of the sutures in the skull, and syndactyly, a fusion of the fingers.

"When I first saw her, I prayed she'd die. They told us she'd need surgery if she lived, and she did."

He told me how he checked his insurance and found it didn't cover birth defects or any surgery relating to them. He went to the March of Dimes, but they could only give 300 dollars if he agreed to accept no other charity. He needed 20,000 dollars. Handicapped Children's Services was going to help, but the state funds were cut off the week before the surgery. He called the governor's office, but they wouldn't talk to him; the lieutenant governor said it was out of his jurisdiction. A senator promised to call back, but later said he had no funds. The caseworker agreed they had tried everything, and it was impossible to get money for the surgery. In desperation he called the state legislature, and finally someone referred him to the state emergency funds. A sympathetic ear heard his case and agreed to pay for the operation.

In two and one-half years, baby Jennifer has had nine surgeries, still needs five or six more, and she still looks extremely abnormal. By the time this dear young man had poured out his problems, we were both in tears. I consoled him, and he cried, "You're the first one who's understood."

I told him I had been debating about a chapter on how to treat people with unusual problems and that I'd prayed for the Lord to direct me. I asked if he would share how people had reacted, and he said, "The most difficult thing is friends who are not supportive. Some wouldn't come to our house anymore for fear it would be contagious." He went on to give examples of what unthinking people had said, as I continued to take notes.

> Strangers ask, "What's wrong with her hands?" A man in a store said, "Good Lord, that child is deformed." One mother pointed and said to her children, "Look at that ugly baby!" Another called her little ones over · and exclaimed, "This baby looks just like E.T.!"

I shared with him how I got a call from a friend when my first little boy was very ill asking if I knew that Lauren arrived at school each day crying. When I asked her, she admitted she was in tears because the children on the bus teased her, calling out, "Your brother's a moron."

"Why didn't you tell me?" I asked.

"I knew you had so much on your mind, I didn't want to upset you anymore."

The young man and I agreed it is often the parent who points out these problems to the children. I asked if I could share his story with others, and he replied, "If it will help one person to be more sensitive to the abnormal child, it will be worth it. Please tell them, 'If you can't say something nice, say nothing.'"

I changed planes in Dallas, boarding the next one and sitting in the same seat location. A lady sat next to me with her eight-year-old son by the aisle. She turned to me and said, "I'm not very happy with this airline. They didn't have three seats together, and my husband had to sit in the back." This sounded like an echo of the first man's words. By then her boy was standing on the seat looking around. As she pulled him down, she asked if I had ever had a "hyperactive boy" like this one. I told her briefly of my two sons, and she said soberly, "You too?"

She then gave me a long history of her 18-year-old retarded and crippled daughter, Ruth, and of the relatives who kept asking her, "What did you do to cause this?" She said children seemed to accept Ruth better than adults, and one child frequently came to the door and asked, "Can I play with your little crippled girl?"

As we shared some of the heartache of a parent with abnormal children, we both agreed: People don't mean to be cruel; they just don't know what to say.

From these two very similar experiences the day after I prayed for direction, I decided I must write on how to handle people with traumas. I mentioned the subject at the next CLASS, and women came up with case histories. It seemed everywhere I went I found new examples. As I sorted through them, I realized that whatever the problem, people did the same things correctly or reacted the same way incorrectly. General principles of positive and negative behavior appeared, and I will share some helpful suggestions with you.

In searching for verses and a title for this chapter, I found 1 Timothy 5:10: "Relieve the afflicted." To make sure I understood the meaning clearly, I looked in the dictionary. *Relieve* means "to free from pain or embarrassment." The afflicted are "those depressed with continual suffering, misfortune or calamity." If you and I are to relieve the afflicted, we must try to ease their pain and not embarrass them. So many people in the cases I was told about had relatives or friends who added guilt to their pain and often hurt or ridiculed them in front of others. If you and I are to relieve the afflicted, we must help anyone we know who is distressed or depressed and who is suffering the loss of a loved one, the misfortune of a divorce, or the calamity of cancer. The list of those with continued suffering is endless. If you and I want to be above average in relieving the afflicted, what should we do?

Not everyone has the gift of mercy or helps, but we can all learn to be sensitive and to care. Let's start with some things *not* to do.

Don'ts

Don't preach or judge. Somehow the Christian world feels called upon to preach to the afflicted. One lady sent me a note saying: "I got tons of advice, well-meant, and strongly delivered, full of certainty, and all conflicting." One woman I know was married to a Baptist preacher. He went through a mid-life crisis and ran off with a young parishioner. The wife did everything she could to pull things back together and was deeply hurt when another pastor told her, "You can be forgiven for the sin of divorce just as you could for murder or stealing." God may lump them all together, but when you are hurting, to be told you're the same as a murderer or thief surely does not relieve the pain.

Don't say, "If you were really a Christian . . ." When my second son was still alive and in the hospital, I would occasionally have a dear little lady come up to me after I spoke about my trauma and say, "If you were really a Christian, you'd have your son home with you where he belongs." Since many of us in crisis are clinging to the Lord Jesus for our strength, it is devastating to have someone question our Christian commitment.

Don't say, "That's not how you're supposed to feel." There's no standard rule on feelings, and in crisis times they may change minute by minute. "You should be happy; he's gone to heaven" does not cheer the bereaved. Whether the victim is weeping or smiling for the moment, being told, "That's not how you're supposed to feel" only makes things worse.

Don't label others as "Tools of the devil." This cliché is used frequently to excuse why things go wrong. "That counselor who told you that was surely a tool of the devil." How do you know? How can it help to pin a label on? How will the designated person feel when he learns what you've called him?

Don't tell horror stories. I remember when my mother was in bed with phlebitis and a friend came in to cheer her up. She told her of a lady who had had the exact same symptoms and had died within an hour. Edith Lanstrom wrote me about coping with a mastectomy: "Do not let other persons invade your environment with negativity. Politely but firmly cut off cancer horror stories. You are already aware of them and don't need to be reminded."

Don't tell of those who had miracles. Equally disturbing are stories of those who were so pure that God healed them, leaving the recipient of the anecdote wondering what's wrong with her. It's good to hold out hope, but be sure not to add the feeling of failure or sin to the person who is already depressed or dying.

Don't write them off. How many times I've been told of permanent rifts in families because one said, "If you do this, I'll write you off"; or to a teenager, "If you ever get pregnant, don't bother to come home"—and she disappears; "If you marry him, I never want to see you again"; "If you don't go to my doctor, I'll wash my hands of your whole problem." Statements like these show we're more interested in having our way than in loving the needy.

When her husband walked out on her, one lady said her mother repeatedly reminded her of two things: "1) There would be no *way* I could survive financially; 2) I had better not expect any help from her." She goes on to say:

> I expect this may be a secret worry in many families. The sweet thing is that her letter this week did contain a small amount of money. I did not want money from her, had never looked to her as a potential source, in no way ever intended to be a burden on her, though she has very comfortable circumstances. The small amount of money meant little one way or the other . . . but the fact that she had wanted to send it, reduced me to tears. As I was reminded of this, I realized this is probably something that others face in one way or another. I have a better source, though . . . a very wealthy Father who has promised to supply all my needs according to His riches!

As I was reading this list of don'ts to a friend's husband yesterday, he stopped me on "Don't write them off" and said,

> That's what I did to a friend in college. I went to Bob Jones University, and my best friend got in

minor trouble. They told him if he wouldn't apologize, they would throw him out. He wouldn't, and they did. I remember saying to him, "If you won't do what they tell you, you realize we can no longer be friends." He left school, and I lost my best friend. I've felt guilty about what I did as a legalistic youth, and I've tried to find words to say I'm sorry, but we've never gotten together. Keep telling people: Don't write them off.

How many well-meaning Christians have written someone off in a moment of poor judgment and lived to regret it. How many grandmothers can't enjoy their grandchildren because they "wrote off" their daughter for some grievous sin and have never been willing to humble themselves and restore fellowship. Oh, dear friends, don't lash out with words you'll have to eat later. If you already have, eat them quickly and restore the "years that the locust hath eaten" (Joel 2:25).

Don't say, "It could be worse." Somehow we feel if we can point out how much worse the circumstances could be, we'll make the person happy. When my mother had a third of her foot cut off because of a malignant tumor, I wasn't cheered by the lady who said, "Just look at it this way: They could have chopped off the whole thing." A young girl gave birth to twins. One of them died at one week old, and she wrote me, "The thing I was told the most was, 'Well, at least you've got the other.'" The grieving for a dead child is not eliminated because there is another one.

When my daughter Lauren lost a child prematurely, some cheered her up by saying, "But think how lucky you are to have little Randy," or "Don't be upset; you're young. You can always have another one."

We often try to tell the afflicted about people who are worse off so they will feel better, but that rarely helps. Whatever the pain of the grieving person, it is maximum to them at that moment.

Don't say, "Pray about it" or "Forget it." To the person in a severe trauma, the saintly words, "Pray about it," are of little comfort. We all know we should pray about our problems and work through them, but there are times when some outside counsel is needed and when "forgetting about it" is not yet possible. A lovely lady I know had been attacked and molested. She had been defenseless and suffered severe emotional consequences. Her church friends told her to "Pray about it and forget it," and quoted Scripture to her. She became severely depressed and, when she finally went to a Christian psychologist, the other women said she was "blaspheming the Holy Spirit" by not trusting in God. They had judged her as a heretic because she sought help in overcoming a problem they had never experienced. Don't cast off every trauma with "Pray about it and forget it." Even if you don't understand the situation or agree with the treatment, be supportive of the individual.

Don't add guilt or search for blame. It is so natural for us to want to step on one who is already down and point out more clearly how he or she got into this situation and whose fault it really is. In divorce problems it becomes almost a Monopoly game of who should advance to "Park Place" and who should "go directly to jail and do not collect $200." One lady described how her pastor expressed concern for her in her impending divorce, but explained that he really had to take her husband's side because "He's one of our biggest contributors." Another woman whose Christian husband had driven off in his new Corvette with a pretty young girl was stripped of her very popular Sunday school class she had taught for 20 years. The pastor's words were, "Obvious failures should not be allowed in leadership positions." A divorcée who was working hard to pull her life together and support her children went to a women's church meeting. The pastor's wife said, "There are two kinds of women here today. You who are married, and you young ones who will be someday." Her message focused on these two types, and those who were divorced or widowed felt ostracized. This lady said, "We are considered nonpersons in a subchurch."

I've never met a divorced person who is proud of it or who found it an exhilarating experience. None of us want it or recommend it, but when it is an accomplished fact, our Christian duty is to relieve the afflicted, not heap guilt on them or show them where they were to blame.

When our families found out our first son was brain-damaged, there was a quick inspection of each side to see if there had been problems like this in the past. Somehow it seemed important to pin blame on the opposite side, but it didn't help me much to be questioned about any ancestors who might have been "a little off." At that time I was asked by several relatives if I had left the baby on the counter and he'd fallen off, and it was inferred that my "gallivanting around and leaving him with sitters" was how he was brain-damaged.

Somehow the more spiritual we think we are, the more we have need to make pronouncements that will indict others. How pathetic that Christians who should give comfort so often feel it's God's appointment to heap guilt on the one in need. When you are the victim of one of life's calamities, you don't need pious platitudes placing blame. Comfort— don't convict.

Don't ignore the problem. The easiest reaction to trauma in others is to ignore it. That way you don't have to view something difficult to look at or get yourself involved in something difficult to handle. In our crisis times more people choose the "ignore the problem" method than any other. If you look the other way, it may go away. And it may, but not because of you. I have talked to so many women who in times of trauma were virtually abandoned by their friends and church. No one wants to see the retarded child, no one wants to get involved in the divorce, no one knows what to do with a rape victim, and no one enjoys weepy widows or dying cancer patients. It's so much easier to look the other way. How do you feel when you're the victim? Like you've got leprosy? Like you've been abandoned? The traumas of life aren't popular. New babies and broken legs we can handle, but we don't want to have to love the unlovable. Dr. John MacDonald writes in his book *When Cancer Strikes* that avoidance is one of the hardest things to take. He relates that when he had a heart operation he had many visits and cards, but when he had cancer, few came. He was dropped from the medical community, and one day when he was feeling well enough to go out, he met a doctor friend who cried out, "My God, it's you! I thought you were dead."

If you wish to be above average, relieve the afflicted. Don't ignore them or their problems. Dr. MacDonald says, "Often the patient welcomes talking about his situation. He loathes talking around it, listening to people who pretend it's not there."[1]

Don't say, "Don't cry." Since we don't know what to do with people who cry, we instinctively tell them not to. We tell them crying is weakness, and to be strong. I was strong through the painful illnesses of my sons. I kept quiet about it. I didn't cry. Many friends never even knew of my problems. I was brave. But oh, how much grief I suppressed!

When my friend Marilyn Murray speaks about her therapy, which brought out many suppressed traumas of her past, she demonstrates with bottles what happens when we suppress our pain. She shows a bottle full of fluid with the cork pushed in and says this represents many of us who have stuffed the hurts and pain under wraps. What happens when the bottle is left in a hot place? It explodes. This is what happens to many of us who have been taught to hold it all in—when things get hot, we explode. It may be a momentary flare-up, a nervous breakdown, or suicide. As I heard her lesson, I decided to write down happenings in my life where I had shoved the problem under the rug or at least had not dealt with my feelings openly. Without much trouble, I had quite a list. How about you? If you found yourself in a hot place, would your bottle explode?

Don't tell people to be brave and not to cry. Sometimes the best thing you can do for people is hold them and let them cry. When Betty Rollins wrote a book on her mastectomy, she titled it *First You Cry*. I'm not suggesting that we all sit around and weep and wail forever, but do realize that crying is a release from all we bottle up inside. And remember: "Weeping may endure for a night, but joy cometh in the morning" (Psalm 30:5).

Why do we find it so difficult to relieve the afflicted? Ask yourself that question. Dr. MacDonald says it's a reflection of our own fear of disease or problems, and it's because we don't know what to say or are unable to handle emotional problems. Many of us have not dealt with our own emotional problems, and therefore are ill-equipped to uplift others. Many of us naturally turn from troubles, and some say, "I've got enough of my own." Some don't want to be associated with anyone who's "not with it" or seen with someone who's on the wrong side of a divorce.

It's a lot easier to ignore problems than deal with them, to condemn rather than understand. But if we want to be above average, what can we do? The next chapter gives suggestions.

Today take the time to listen patiently to a friend in need.

ADDITIONAL CHALLENGES FOR MEN:

Dealing with pain and problems is much harder for men than for women. By nature, women have nurturing spirits, while men have been taught that only sissies cry. When my two sons were dying, I sat and held them, rocked them, kissed them, and cried over them. Fred couldn't look at them. To him having two sons who had no brain activity was a blot on his manhood. How could he have produced these genetically deficient babies? What was wrong with him?

Often this is the response men have when faced with a handicapped or retarded child. Statistics vary, but all show that a high percentage of couples who have abnormal babies get divorced, usually because the husband can't deal with the thought that he has produced something that is far from perfect. It's easier to turn away and not be reminded daily of this personal embarrassment.

Gratefully, as Fred committed his life to the Lord in this time of despair, he received the gift of compassion and today spends much of his time relieving the afflicted.

The Lord will give a man a compassionate heart if he asks Him. It's not a sign of weakness to care for those who are hurting.

Be sure you don't stifle the natural emotions of your sons. Let them cry when they're hurt, tell them you understand and care. Don't make them stuff their feelings in a bottle which will someday explode and shatter all over their family.

Reread the don'ts in this chapter, and then move on to the dos.

Start today to feel for others. Relieve the afflicted.

It takes so little to be above average.

CHAPTER TWENTY-NINE

Comfort Ye
My People

*Comfort ye, comfort ye my people,
saith your God.*

—Isaiah 40:1

*T*o comfort is to "cheer in time of grief or trouble, to relieve pain." God has instructed us to cheer His people in time of trouble, and yet it is so difficult to do. One lady excused herself by saying, "It's just not my gift." It's not mine either. I'm so poor at dealing with sickness that my family says I have a "lack of nurseness." But God did not say, "Comfort ye my people if you have a feel for it, if it's your gift, if it's convenient." In Psalm 69:20 is a plaintive verse: "I looked for some to take pity, but there was none; and for comforters, but I found none." This verse describes some of those in our Christian community: People with buckets of burdens looking for people with armloads of answers but finding few real comforters, few who are ready to give cheer in time of grief. This lack of desire to help is especially noticed in the areas of "unpopular problems" such as rape, incest, and child molestation.

Years ago I thought those troubles were either fiction or far away in another town. I had read the accepted figure that one out of four girls by the age of 16 is the victim of some form of sexual molestation, but I didn't think I knew any of them. The first time Marilyn Murray spoke on this subject during CLASS at the Crystal Cathedral, I was dumbfounded when out of a group of 80 above-average women, 25 came to Marilyn and poured out their traumas. In San Antonio, out of 180 women, 60 identified themselves as victims, and in Walnut Creek, 35 out of 110.

Suddenly, I had to face the fact that good Christian women have had the same proportion of sexual molestation as the national average. Marilyn had to stay extra days in each city to "comfort my people." As she listened to them, the majority started by saying, "I've never told this to anyone before." Why? Because they *knew* no one would ever understand. As Marilyn shared her experience, she pushed buttons on women who had been waiting to find someone who would understand, who could comfort them in their hidden grief. All had suppressed their feelings. Those few who had sought Christian counsel had been told to pray about it and forget it. One popular answer given to a grieving victim is "Forgive the offender and then move on. Once you've forgiven, you'll feel much better." Some had been instructed to never mention this to anyone again. Some were told that rape victims ask for it, and some that "I'm sure it's all in your head." None of these answers is a comfort to one whose bottle is about to explode.

While laypeople are often not equipped to counsel trauma victims, we can at least be sensitive to the desperate needs around us and realize there are many heavy hearts with hidden burdens.

Fred and I put together our book *Get a Life Without the Strife* to give people a tool to analyze the source of their own problems and to be of help to others. It contains a series of tests starting with personality types, then goes on to deal with stress, maturity, rejection, and grief. There is a section on how to tell if your child has been abused, if you have suffered hidden trauma, and if you might be MPD (Multiple Personality Disorder). This book of tests will help you diagnose where your own problems come from and guide others to truth about themselves.

God wants us to have our eyes open, to comfort His people, to relieve the afflicted. Above-average women are all in demand. Isaiah 50:4 says, "The Lord GOD hath given me the tongue of the learned, that I should know how to speak a word in season to him that is weary." What can we do to comfort the depressed, the defenseless, the diseased, the dying?

Try to understand. Even though we may never have been through the causal experience of the distressed person, we can try to understand. We can tell the individual of some similar feeling we've had, even if from a different set of circumstances. Almost everyone who is distraught thinks at the moment that no one understands. People relate best to someone who's been there. Because I've had marriage problems, lost two brain-damaged sons, and experienced depression, women know I'll understand in these areas. Because Marilyn was the victim of a sexual attack as a child, women see for the first time someone who will understand.

Because Barbara Bueler was the victim of a shooting and also lost her home and all her belongings in a fire, women know she will have compassion. Because Francine Jackson comes from a broken home, has experienced repeated rejections, and has risen to the challenge of stepfamily living, women flock to her for comfort.

A dear young girl named Sally approached me after I gave my testimony in Birmingham telling me about her 16-month-old baby still in the hospital from birth with multiple brain-damage problems. Sally was emotionally drained, felt she needed to get out of town, and was sure no one understood her. Later she wrote me:

> I want to express my deepest thank you for understanding and giving the advice that it wouldn't be so wrong of me to want to get away from the situation with my daughter. So many people do not understand why I would leave this baby, but I absolutely have to for my own health. I do not want to upset you by making you dwell on the situation with your two sons; you have gone through it, survived it, are a very strong woman to go on sharing it in your conferences, books, et cetera. I know how much it hurts to tell others about this type of thing. Just think of it like this—you are reaching out to people who have sick kids like me. You have helped me already. May God give you as much strength as you need to go on sharing with others.

The most constant statement I hear in marriage counseling is, "He doesn't understand." This statement means he "doesn't comprehend the nature or the character" of the person or the problem. If we can only try to understand, we will comfort people.

Listen. Once people think we understand or at least want to understand, they will pour out their problems, and all we have to do is listen. We don't have to be brilliant or even have a three-step solution; we only have to listen. No one listens to anyone anymore; they're all too busy. So if we just listen, we become a devoted friend. Everywhere I go—on planes, in lines, in the ladies' room—I find people who give me their buckets of burdens. I don't have to make up case histories; I only have to listen. They can sense that I care, and they talk. Sometimes a stranger after pouring out a whole life upon me will suddenly say, "I don't know why I told you all this." She had to tell it to someone, and I was there.

My dear friend Frances Thomas in Dallas coped with cancer for many years. When I asked her how people could be of help to her, she replied: "The key to the whole thing is to *listen*. Some days we want to talk about it, and some days we don't, so be sensitive."

Frances, who says her aim in life is "to be attuned to what God wants me to do for Him," says her "greatest asset is the love of godly friends."

Be available to listen. Long-term patients especially need to have someone sit beside them. Doctors say terminal patients don't fear death so much as they fear being alone.

Sometimes our greatest ministry to one in bereavement or one waiting through a loved one's surgery is to just be there and be sensitive. The poet John Milton said, "They also serve who only stand and wait."[1]

Do something specific. When we try to understand others' problems and are willing to listen, we help their hurting hearts. Now what can we do for them physically?

Obviously, each problem has different needs, but let's look at some practical solutions. Average people often say, "If there's anything I can do, let me know." Above-average people do something specific.

At the time of a death, drop in to express your love, call to let them know you care, or visit the funeral home. Send flowers, a memorial gift, or a card. Always add a personal note expressing some warm thoughts about the deceased. Tana Reiff, in an article in McCall's magazine, writes:

> Of the many personal visits and cards and letters my mother received at the time of my father's death, my mother says, "I was particularly comforted by those that recalled a special memory of how my husband's life influenced theirs. It was wonderful to hear for the first time stories about things he had done years ago."[2]

Elizabeth Swank, who attended the Fort Worth CLASS, wrote:

> My husband, after fifty years in the ministry (forty-three as pastor of one church) died suddenly last fall. I received hundreds of cards and letters, expressing sympathy. I soon saw that most fell into one of two categories. One was the "devotional thought" with Scripture—pointing to the joys of heaven, etc. The second which I found much more comforting were the "I will-miss-him-too" expressions which included some humorous story or some generous act involving my husband. They mostly ended with "I'm so glad I knew him." Certainly, I'll remember this when I try to comfort others.

If you bring food to a family, this gesture is always appreciated whether it is because of a death, a hospital stay, sickness at home, or just some bad news. Putting the effort into cooking something yourself always has an uplifting effect. One winter when I had a brief bout with pneumonia, Lynn Hall, a young mother in our church, called to say she heard I was sick and she was bringing me dinner. It was the first time in years that anyone had done this for me, and I was excitedly shocked. I'll never forget that catered dinner and that dear woman who cared enough to prepare it.

When I was visiting the home of Joann and Mel Turner in Dallas, they had a friend whose husband was in the hospital. The friend had been at the hospital constantly and had not been able to keep her house in order. I was amazed when Joann had her own cleaning lady accompany her to clean the friend's house. At dinner that night Joann said there had been so much to do that both of them had worked on the house all day. To me that kind of service for a friend is above average.

When my babies were ill and I had been told there was no hope, I didn't care if I lived another day. Going to one more doctor to get the same answers was sometimes more than I thought I could handle. During that period I had one friend who called every morning at 9 A.M. Louise Knaut checked in to see if I had any needs that day, and if I did, she filled them. She ran errands and picked my girls up at school, but most of all she went with me to my doctor appointments. She never put any pressure on me. Although she was a very busy woman, she sat patiently with me in many waiting rooms. That's an above-average friend!

When Jan Craton at Fort Worth was going through an unwanted divorce, much of the Christian community looked the other way. I asked her if there had been one person who had been helpful, and she answered:

At the top of the list must be my precious friend who is closer than a sister to me. She just stood by me, and came to be with me at any hour of the day or the night, and no matter how impossible I was, no matter if I cried or got angry, no matter what, she just hung in there and never took offense, and kept on loving me, and kept on enduring the pain with me . . . talk about unconditional love! That same friend literally took me by the hand, and led me back to my Bible, which I had lost the habit of reading. She just said, in desperation, not knowing what else to do with me, "Come on, Jan, let's read." And those words just leaped off the page at me. They just began to nourish and strengthen me like cool water to a starving person. I had read the Bible all my life, and I didn't know how wonderful it was until then.

When Wendy Bergren of Walnut Creek was a young mother struggling to beat cancer, many people volunteered to help. From her lengthy illness she compiled what had been the most meaningful ministries to her. She wrote 20 suggestions including:

Cook a dinner and bring it in disposable containers.
Bake cookies and bring them frozen.
Offer to babysit.
Wrap presents for my children to take to parties.
Take snapshots of my children.
Encourage your husband to visit mine.

Use your creativity and custom-make your kindnesses to fit the needs of the people.

Follow through. Don't tell anyone you will do something and then not do it. Idle words such as, "I'll call you in a few weeks" may be the hope a person clings to that is shattered when you in your busy life forget to call. Some say they have a "great book" that will help, and then don't bring it. Some say, "You will love my apple pie," and don't bake one. The average person means well, but it takes someone above average to follow through.

Hug and touch. Many times we are afraid we won't know what to say at a funeral, and so we don't go or we sneak out. At that point the family doesn't want a fascinating monologue; they just want to know you cared enough to come. A touch on the hand or an arm around the shoulders is far more helpful than a few clever sentences about how impressed you are with the casket.

Cancer victims especially need to be hugged or patted since many receive vibrations from friends that they are contagious. Those of us with retarded or abnormal children want a friend who will hold that child instead of turn from him. Some people can't and we understand, but we will love the friend who will love our child.

Continue to include. The hardest thing to bear for people who have lost a mate through death or divorce is that their friends frequently drop them from the social roster. Since they no longer fit the norm, they are left out. It takes an above average person to care enough to be creative and include the single friend.

Hold confidences. You wouldn't think this point would need to be made in Christian circles, but I hear so frequently of a person who poured her heart out at a moment of trauma only to hear it all back a few weeks later from a different source. I've known pastors who have told their wives, who have told their prayer group, who have told their friends. When people are already distraught and have shared confidences they've never told a soul before, they fall apart when they find their life on the prayer chain.

Share Scripture. At the moment of crisis most people don't want a saintly friend reminding them that "all things work together for good to those who love the Lord and are called according to His purpose." Twenty years down the line I can see that God has taken the tragedies of my life and used them to bring me to my knees and to the Savior, but I wouldn't have enjoyed hearing it back then. Whatever the problem, be sensitive to when you should share a Scripture with the needy friend. Some want words of hope immediately, and others, who have decided for the moment that there is no God, will be angered or turned off. God is not pushy, and He will give you direction at the right time.

Love and accept. Even though we all preach unconditional love, we have trouble really living it. We get along fine with those who agree with us and live according to our standards, but it's difficult not to judge the sinner and condemn the fallen. If we know more than ten verses by heart, we feel called upon to stand with Moses and discern with Solomon. We tend to say, "I'll love you if . . ." and "I'll accept you when . . ."

What was Jesus' attitude toward the person caught in moral problems? In John 8:1-11 we read a simple story. Jesus is teaching a Bible study. He has no doubt worked on it all week and has passed out the study guides. He has everyone's attention focused on the heart of His message, when the real spiritual giants who know everything walk in. They haven't had time for learning from the Lord because they are the "Secret Spirit Squad" sent out to spy. They try to turn up a few sinners a day to help purify the church. Today they have a biggie—a woman caught in adultery, "in the very act." They know Jesus would want this important information even though He's in the middle of teaching, so they barge right in and set her in the midst of the group. In case Jesus has forgotten the rules, they remind Him such a sinner should be stoned to death.

But Jesus doesn't overreact. Instead He looks at this legalistic lot and says, "He that is without sin among you, let him first cast a stone at her." Can you imagine the soul-searching that went on at that time? As they each listen to the drip, drip, drip of their conscience, one by one they drop away. Jesus has His head down; He doesn't care to check who leaves in what order. When they are all gone, He looks up and asks the woman where her accusers are. He doesn't give her a lecture; He doesn't recite the Ten Commandments.

Can you imagine what we might be led to do at such a moment, faced with a proven sinner caught in the very act? Could we resist a few condemning verses? Wouldn't we lead her in the sinner's prayer? Would we carry her to a confession booth, call the church elders, or capture the moment on film? Would we pull her down to the sand and have her kneel over a rock of repentance?

You can be sure we would have made an example of her, if not an exhibit. But what did Jesus do? He quietly asked, "Hath no man condemned thee?"

She answered, "No man, Lord." And Jesus said to her, "Neither do I condemn thee: go and sin no more."

Jesus loved her and accepted her as she was. He didn't preach, judge, or say, "If you were really a Christian, you wouldn't have done this." He didn't blame it on the devil or tell horror stories of what happened to others caught in adultery. He forgave her, and He comforted His people. Jesus was and is and evermore will be above average! How about you and me?

Today make that call you have been putting off because you "don't know what to say."

ADDITIONAL CHALLENGES FOR MEN:

To "comfort" sounds like a woman's job, like a motherly duty, but God was speaking to men when he said, "Comfort ye my people." There are two ways in which men can be part of God's comforting plan. The first and easiest is to be supportive of your wife as she cares for others. When she wishes to take food to a family in need, take it for her (or at least don't tell her she shouldn't do it). When she wants to visit a sick friend in the hospital, don't say, "Why don't you stay home with me where you belong?" Help her to be a comforter.

Second, be open to care for others yourself, especially in areas where you have personal experience. If you have professional skills, offer them to your pastor to help out those who are in need and have no money. We know lawyers who give a night a month to answer legal questions for the church body, doctors who give free service to cases sent by the pastor, dentists who give a week or more a year to go to Mexico and work on teeth that would have been neglected.

Ask the Lord where He would like you to serve. He tells us He is "the Father of mercies, and the God of all comfort." He says He comforts us in all our tribulation "that we may be able to comfort them which are in any trouble, by the comfort wherewith we ourselves are comforted of God" (2 Corinthians 1:4).

In simple terms, God will use each one of us who is will-ing to comfort others who are going through the same prob-lems we've been through ourselves.

My husband in the early days of our marriage was far more interested in business than in people. He could never have been considered to be a comforter or even a listener to people's problems. Yet today he spends hours a week listen-ing and comforting. Why? Because, through prayer, Fred uncovered the molestation he had experienced as a child. Through continued daily written prayer, Fred was healed of his pain and now comforts others and gives them hope.

God uses human beings who have had difficult experi-ences to comfort others who are going through similar prob-lems.

Our God is a creative God, and He will customize a personal ministry for all those who are willing to care for others. He also guarantees that He won't call us to any action that He won't equip us to do.

Be open to the Lord's leading in your life.

Comfort ye My people.

It takes so little to be above average.

PART VIII

It Takes So Little to Pray Above Average

CHAPTER THIRTY

Come Home
to Prayer

*D*o all of us pray above average? If average in-
cludes everyone in the world, then if you pray
at all, you pray above average. But how could
we do better?

As we approach the turn of the century, there is a renewed
interest in prayer. Why? The reason is because all else has
failed. In this country we have believed in ourselves and in our
ability to rise from nothing to greatness. We started as an odd
collection of pilgrims seeking religious freedom and as fugitives
from the law of other countries. Like a child who has run away
from home, we wanted to show our Father we could make it on
our own. With many struggles we grew up and became the
greatest. The United States of America has been on top with
its form of government, its military, its resources, its education,
its morals, its freedoms, its families, its individuals. When
you're the best, you don't need outside help.

What has happened, however, in the nineties. Our government has been hurt by scandal, our cities are unmanageable

and on the verge of bankruptcy, our leaders fear for their lives, and drugs have altered the future of many of our youth.

Our military is no longer the superpower we once believed it was, being in the service does not bear the patriotic fervor it once did, and bases are being closed all over the country.

Our resources are not sufficient for our needs. Our economy has been manipulated by outside influences, and many of our manufactured products are not competitive on the world market.

Our education system is at its worst point in history. As I quoted earlier, the Commission on Excellence found only "pockets of excellence" to praise, and reported the current school population to be the first generation in our history to know less than its parents.

Our moral fibers have been frazzled. As a nation we have abandoned any semblance of moral standards. We've grown up; we're out on our own; we don't have to live by Father's house rules anymore. In this time of sexual freedom, we have seen more mental breakdowns, emotional traumas, and teenage pregnancies than ever before. As one headline lamented, "There's no freedom in the free lifestyle." In my seminars filled with outstanding Christian women, we find victims of rape, incest, and molestation; we find mothers of drug abusers, homosexuals, runaways, and cultists; we find wives of abusive men, adulterers, and alcoholics.

American families are falling apart, and the Christian world is no exception. Infidelity is now so acceptable we're hardly shocked when we hear of it, and the ease of divorce has made marriage commitment a temporary condition.

When we run out of faith in the institutions we grew up believing in, that brings each one of us down to me and, "I'm not even sure of me. I'm lonely, insecure, and fearful. Where can I turn for help?"

As a country we grew up to greatness; we got fat and rich. We ran away from restrictions, plunged into pleasure, and sought self-gratification. Now, like the prodigal son, we've run the gamut, we've run out of resources and we want to come home. We're finally desperate enough to admit we've made mistakes and to confess them to our Father.

Will He forgive us? Will He take us back? Does He hear us knocking at the gate?

What did He do for the prodigal son? In the beginning of the parable, the son was an integral part of the family. He belonged, he ate with the family and enjoyed the family fellowship. He was a child who depended upon his father and communed with him daily. In comparing him with ourselves, we need to ask ourselves if we really belong to the Father's family. Have we as individuals accepted the invitation of the Father to belong to the family of God?

"As many as received him, to them gave he power to become the sons of God" (John 1:12).

The invitation is always out; the door is always open. We need only to say, "Lord Jesus, I accept Your invitation. I'm lonely and want to belong to the family of God. I know I've not spent time with You, and I want to change. I'm grateful that You have the power to adopt me into Your family, and I thank You for what You're going to do in my life. Amen."

As the son in the story grew up, his father gave him a free will to choose what kind of a life he wished to live. The son, thinking he didn't need the father anymore and that the ways of the world sounded more exciting, took his portion of the inheritance and left.

How many of us, after becoming part of the family of God, have made poor choices? Have felt the world and its ways seemed preferable to the straight-and-narrow road? Have compromised our standards and failed to keep in touch with the Father?

Once the son had spent his money, his fickle friends no longer knew him. They went off to richer companions.

He was lonely and hungry and began to reminisce about the warmth of the father's home. He didn't want to go back and admit his mistakes, but he had the faith that his father loved him and would welcome him back. Scripture tells us: "When he was yet a great way off, his father saw him, and had compassion, and ran, and fell on his neck, and kissed him" (Luke 15:20).

When all else fails, we can come home: "And it shall come to pass that before they call, I will answer; and while they are yet speaking, I will hear" (Isaiah 65:24).

Before we call, our Father hears us. The prodigal son confessed his sins, and his father had an instant celebration. He didn't give him a lecture at the gate or say, "I told you so." He brought out the best robe, put a ring on his hand and shoes on his feet. He killed the fatted calf; they ate and were merry because what was lost had been found.

How about you? Have you run away from home? Have you gone to the end of the road? Have the world and its pleasures failed you? Are you ready to come home to your Father? Do you want to ask His forgiveness? Some of you may ask: "How do I pray?" You remember the prodigal son who had "wasted his substance on riotous living" and then "came to himself" and returned home. He didn't bring a big list of requests. He didn't give a pompous prayer. He just came to the gate with a humble and contrite heart and asked his father to take him back.

How about you? Have you been praying below-average prayers? Have you been asking for favors, presenting conditions, or calling for help when you're still in the far country? Come home. Come home! "Draw nigh to God, and he will draw nigh to you" (James 4:8).

In our personal experience, Fred and I have found that we can come nearer to God when we put our prayers in writing. Here is an opportunity to start in a simple way to come home to the Father. As you write to the Lord, put down the first thoughts that come to you. Don't try for fancy phrases, just write!

Come Home

Dear Father, I've come home. Here's where I've been:

_____

_____

_____

Here's what I've been doing:

_____

_____

_____

Here's the trouble I've gotten into:

_____

_____

_____

I know You are always "nigh unto them that are of a broken heart" (Psalm 34:18).

I know You are a "God at hand . . . and not a God afar off," and I'm home (Jeremiah 23:23).

Call Out

Dear Lord, I know You are standing and knocking at the door of my heart. I want You to come in and sup with me. The world has failed me. I'm alone. You've told me in the past, "Call to me, and I will answer you, and I will show you great and mighty things which you do not know." Father, I don't know much. Tell me great and mighty things. I'm willing to listen. "I cried unto the LORD with my voice" (Psalm 142:1). I'm waiting for Your reply.

Confess

Dear Father,
I've wasted much of my life in:

_____

_____

_____

I've said unkind things to:

_____

_____

_____

I need to forgive:

_____

_____

_____

You've told me if I confess my sins You are faithful and just to forgive me and to cleanse me from all unrighteousness (1 John 1:9).

I confess:

_____

_____

_____

As the prodigal son was willing to come home when he realized how far away he was from the protection of his father, so we need to return to our Lord, our God, our Father. We need to write our prayers daily, as we are doing now, as intimate letters to a Father who loves us and has welcomed us back. We need to call out to Him and confess that we have been disobedient children who have seen the error of our ways. As we write to Him and share the hurts of our hearts, He will respond and we can celebrate together. Here's a sample prayer, a small beginning as we, the prodigal sons, return.

Celebrate

Dear Father, I've come home, I've called out. I've confessed. Bring me into Your home and let's celebrate together. I feel Your warmth and Your welcome. "Let my prayer be set forth before thee as incense" (Psalm 141:2). As we sit at Your table and eat the fatted calf, I see Jesus Christ at Your right hand, making intercession for me (Romans 8:34). While I've been away, He's been there beside You, putting in a good word for me. Let's celebrate, for he who was lost has returned.

Thank You for Your mantle which You've placed over my shoulders that I might never be cold again. Thank You for the ring of love You've placed on my finger that I may reach out a caring hand and relieve the afflicted. Thank You for the shoes on my feet that I might walk in Your path and spread Your words wherever I go.

Dear Father:

> I've come home.
> I've called out.
> I've confessed, now
> Let's celebrate, in Jesus' precious name.
>   Amen.

What a Father we have:

> Above heaven and earth
> Above every living creature
> *Above average!*

Today begin that journey back to the warmth of the Father with written prayer.

ADDITIONAL CHALLENGES FOR MEN:

So often, men feel the spiritual life of the family is the duty of the wife, that prayer and Bible study is women's work. Yet, in Scripture, Father God is constantly speaking to men and challenging them to lead their families, to protect their wives, and to share God's Word with their children. "Teach them diligently," the Bible says. It doesn't say to tell your wife to teach them. Do it when you sit, walk, lie down, or rise up (Deuteronomy 6:7).

In 1 Peter 3:7, Peter tells the men to live with their wives according to biblical knowledge, to treat them with honor and respect as heirs together of the inheritance from the Father, so that their prayers will not be hindered.

God the Father is looking today for men who are willing to rise up, to come home, to call out to God, to confess their sins and their lack of spiritual knowledge, and to give their families positive leadership and a reason to celebrate.

All else has failed. Come home.

Second Chronicles 7:14 sums up the challenge for Christians today:

> "If my people, which are called by my name [those who are part of His family], shall humble themselves, and pray, and seek my face [come home, call out], and turn from their wicked ways [confess and change]; then will I hear from heaven [will welcome you home], and will forgive their sin, and will heal their land."

What a celebration there will be!
Men, it's up to you to

Come home
Call out
Confess and
Celebrate, so that the Father will heal our land.

Because of who He is, *it takes so little for you to be above average.*

Appendix

Personality Test Word Definitions
(Adapted From Personality Patterns by Lana Bateman)

STRENGTHS

1. **ADAPTABLE.** Easily fits and is comfortable in any situation.
   ADVENTUROUS. One who will take on new and daring enterprises with a determination to master them.
   ANALYTICAL. Likes to examine the parts for their logical and proper relationships.
   ANIMATED. Full of life, lively use of hand, arm, and face gestures.

2. **PEACEFUL.** Seems undisturbed and tranquil and retreats from any form of strife.
   PERSISTENT. Sees one project through to its completion before starting another.
   PERSUASIVE. Convinces through logic and fact rather than charm or power.
   PLAYFUL. Full of fun and good humor.

3. **SUBMISSIVE.** Easily accepts any other's point of view or desire with little need to assert his own opinion.
   SELF-SACRIFICING. Willingly gives up his own personal being for the sake of, or to meet the needs of, others.
   SOCIABLE. One who sees being with others as an opportunity to be cute and entertaining rather than as a challenge or business opportunity.
   STRONG-WILLED. One who is determined to have his own way.

4. **CONSIDERATE.** Having regard for the needs and feelings of others.
   CONTROLLED. Has emotional feelings but rarely displays them.
   COMPETITIVE. Turns every situation, happening, or game into a contest and always plays to win!
   CONVINCING. Can win you over to anything through the sheer charm of his personality.

5. **REFRESHING.** Renews and stimulates or makes others feel good.
   RESPECTFUL. Treats others with deference, honor, and esteem.
   RESERVED. Self-restraint in expression of emotion or enthusiasm.
   RESOURCEFUL. Able to act quickly and effectively in virtually all situations.

6. **SATISFIED.** A person who easily accepts any circumstance or situation.
   SENSITIVE. Intensively cares about others, and what happens.
   SELF-RELIANT. An independent person who can fully rely on his own capabilities, judgment, and resources.
   SPIRITED. Full of life and excitement.

7. **PLANNER.** Prefers to work out a detailed arrangement beforehand for the accomplishment of project or goal, and prefers involvement with the planning stages and the finished product rather than the carrying out of the task.
   PATIENT. Unmoved by delay, remains calm and tolerant.
   POSITIVE. Knows it will turn out right if he's in charge.
   PROMOTER. Urges or compels others to go along, join, or invest through the charm of his own personality.

8. **SURE.** Confident, rarely hesitates or wavers.
SPONTANEOUS. Prefers all of life to be impulsive, unpremeditated activity, not restricted by plans.
SCHEDULED. Makes and lives according to a daily plan; dislikes his plan to be interrupted.
SHY. Quiet, doesn't easily instigate a conversation.

9. **ORDERLY.** A person who has a methodical, systematic arrangement of things.
OBLIGING. Accommodating. One who is quick to do it another's way.
OUTSPOKEN. Speaks frankly and without reserve.
OPTIMISTIC. Sunny disposition who convinces himself and others that everything will turn out all right.

10. **FRIENDLY.** A responder rather than an initiator; seldom starts a conversation.
FAITHFUL. Consistently reliable, steadfast, loyal, and devoted, sometimes beyond reason.
FUNNY. Sparkling sense of humor that can make virtually any story into an hilarious event.
FORCEFUL. A commanding personality whom others would hesitate to take a stand against.

11. **DARING.** Willing to take risks; fearless, bold.
DELIGHTFUL. A person who is upbeat and fun to be with.
DIPLOMATIC. Deals with people tactfully, sensitively, and patiently.
DETAILED. Does everything in proper order with a clear memory of all the things that happened.

12. **CHEERFUL.** Consistently in good spirits and promoting happiness in others.
CONSISTENT. Stays emotionally on an even keel, responding as one might expect.
CULTURED. One whose interests involve both intellectual and artistic pursuits, such as theater, symphony, ballet.
CONFIDENT. Self-assured and certain of own ability and success.

13. **IDEALISTIC.** Visualizes things in their perfect form and has a need to measure up to that standard himself.
INDEPENDENT. Self-sufficient, self-supporting, self-confident and seems to have little need of help.
INOFFENSIVE. A person who never says or causes anything unpleasant or objectionable.
INSPIRING. Encourages others to work, join, or be involved and makes the whole thing fun.

14. **DEMONSTRATIVE** Openly expresses emotion, especially affection, and doesn't hesitate to touch others while speaking to them.
DECISIVE. A person with quick, conclusive, judgment-making ability.
DRY HUMOR. Exhibits "dry wit," usually humorous one-liners which can be sarcastic in nature.
DEEP. Intense and often introspective with a distaste for surface conversation and pursuits.

15. **MEDIATOR.** Consistently finds himself in the role of reconciling differences in order to avoid conflict.

   MUSICAL. Participates in or has a deep appreciation for music, is committed to music as an artform, rather than the fun of performance.

   MOVER. Driven by a need to be productive; a leader whom others follow; finds it difficult to sit still.

   MIXES EASILY. Loves a party and can't wait to meet everyone in the room; never meets a stranger.

16. **THOUGHTFUL.** A considerate person who remembers special occasions and is quick to make a kind gesture.

   TENACIOUS. Holds on firmly, stubbornly, and won't let got until the goal is accomplished.

   TALKER. Constantly talking, generally telling funny stories and entertaining everyone around, feeling the need to fill the silence in order to make others comfortable.

   TOLERANT. Easily accepts the thoughts and ways of others without the need to disagree with or change them.

17. **LISTENER.** Always seems willing to hear what you have to say.

   LOYAL. Faithful to a person, ideal, or job, sometimes beyond reason.

   LEADER. A natural-born director who is driven to be in charge and often finds it difficult to believe that anyone else can do the job as well.

   LIVELY. Full of life, vigorous, energetic.

18. **CONTENTED.** Easily satisfied with what he has; rarely envious.

   CHIEF. Commands leadership and expects people to follow.

   CHARTMAKER. Organizes life, tasks, and problem solving by making lists, forms, or graphs.

   CUTE. Precious, adorable, center of attention.

19. **PERFECTIONIST.** Places high standards on himself, and often on others, desiring that everything be in proper order at all times.

   PLEASANT. Easygoing, easy to be around, easy to talk with.

   PRODUCTIVE. Must constantly be working or achieving; often finds it very difficult to rest.

   POPULAR. Life of the party and therefore much desired as a party guest.

20. **BOUNCY.** A bubbly, lively personality, full of energy.

   BOLD. Fearless, daring, forward, unafraid of risk.

   BEHAVED. Consistently desires to conduct himself within the realm of what he f eels is proper.

   BALANCED. Stable, middle-of-the-road personality, not subject to sharp highs or lows.

WEAKNESS

21. **BLANK.** A person who shows little facial expression or emotion.
22. **BASHFUL.** Shrinks from getting attention, resulting from self-consciousness.

BRASSY. Showy, flashy, comes on strong, too loud.

BOSSY. Commanding, domineering, sometimes overbearing in adult relationships.

22. **UNDISCIPLINED.** A person whose lack of order permeates most every area of his life.

    UNSYMPATHETIC. Finds it difficult to relate to the problems or hurts of others.

    UNENTHUSIASTIC. Tends to not get excited, often feeling it won't work anyway.

    UNFORGIVING. One who has difficulty releasing or forgetting a hurt or injustice done to him, apt to hold onto a grudge.

23. **RETICENT.** Unwilling to get, or struggles against getting, involved, especially when complex.

    RESENTFUL. Often holds ill feelings as a result of real or imagined offenses.

    RESISTANT. Strives, works against, or hesitates to accept any other way but his own.

    REPETITIOUS. Retells stories and incidents to entertain you without realizing he has already told the story several times before; is constantly needing something to say.

24. **FUSSY.** Insistent over petty matters or details, calling great attention to trivial details.

    FEARFUL. Often experiences feelings of deep concern, apprehension, or anxiousness.

    FORGETFUL. Lack of memor, which is usually tied to a lack of discipline and not bothering to mentally record things that aren't fun.

    FRANK. Straightforward, outspoken, and doesn't mind telling you exactly what he thinks.

25. **IMPATIENT.** A person who finds it difficult to endure irritation or wait for others.

    INSECURE. One who is apprehensive or lacks confidence.

    INDECISIVE. The person who finds it difficult to make any decision at all. (Not the personality that labors long over each decision in order to make the perfect one.)

    INTERRUPTS. A person who is more of a talker than a listener, who starts speaking without even realizing someone else is already speaking.

26. **UNPOPULAR.** A person whose intensity and demand for perfection can push others away.

    UNINVOLVED. Has no desire to listen or become interested in clubs, groups, activities, or other people's lives.

    UNPREDICTABLE: May be ecstatic one moment and down the next, or willing to help but then disappears, or promises to come but forgets to show up.

    UNAFFECTIONATE. Finds it difficult to verbally or physically demonstrate tenderness openly.

27. **HEADSTRONG.** Insists on having his own way.

    HAPHAZARD. Has no consistent way of doing things.

    HARD to PLEASE. A person whose standards are set so high that it is difficult to ever satisfy them.

    HESITANT. Slow to get moving and hard to get involved.

28. **PLAIN.** A middle-of-the-road personality without highs or lows and showing little, if any, emotion.

   PESSIMISTIC. While hoping for the best, this person generally sees the down side of a situation first.

   PROUD. One with great self-esteem who sees himself as always right and the best person for the job.

   PERMISSIVE. Allows others (including children) to do as they please in order to keep from being disliked.

29. **ANGERED EASILY.** One who has a childlike flash-in-the-pan temper that expresses itself in tantrum style and is over and forgotten almost instantly.

   AIMLESS. Not a goal-setter with little desire to be one.

   ARGUMENTATIVE. Incites arguments generally because he is certain he is right no matter what the situation may be.

   ALIENATED. Easily feels estranged from others often because of insecurity or fear that others don't really enjoy his company.

30. **NAIVE.** Simple and child-like perspective, lacking sophistication or comprehension of what the deeper levels of life are really about.

   NEGATIVE ATTITUDE. One whose attitude is seldom positive and is often able to see only the down or dark side of each situation.

   NERVY. Full of confidence, fortitude, and sheer guts, often in a negative sense.

   NONCHALANT. Easy-going, unconcerned, indifferent.

31. **WORRIER.** Consistently feels uncertain, troubled, or anxious.

   WITHDRAWN. A person who pulls back to himself and needs a great deal of alone or isolation time.

   WORKAHOLIC. An aggressive goal-setter who must be constantly productive and feels very guilty when resting, is not driven by a need for perfection or completion but by a need for accomplishment and reward.

   WANTS CREDIT. Thrives on the credit or approval of others. As an entertainer this person feeds on the applause, laughter, and/or acceptance of an audience.

32. **TOO SENSITIVE.** Overly introspective and easily offended when misunderstood.

   TACTLESS. Sometimes expresses himself in a somewhat offensive and inconsiderate way.

   TIMID. Shrinks from difficult situations.

   TALKATIVE. An entertaining, compulsive talker who finds it difficult to listen.

33. **DOUBTFUL.** Characterized by uncertainty and lack of confidence that it will ever work out.

   DISORGANIZED. Lack of ability to ever get life in order.

   DOMINEERING. Compulsively takes control of situations and/or people, usually telling others what to do.

   DEPRESSED. A person who feels down much of the time.

34. **INCONSISTENT.** Erratic, contradictory, with actions and emotions not based on logic.

   INTROVERT. A person whose thoughts and interest are directed inward, lives within himself.

INTOLERANT. Appears unable to withstand or accept another's attitudes, point of view, or way of doing things.

INDIFFERENT. A person to whom most things don't matter one way or the other.

35. **MESSY.** Living in a state of disorder, unable to find things.

MOODY. Doesn't get very high emotionally, but easily slips into low lows, often when feeling unappreciated.

MUMBLES. Will talk quietly under the breath when pushed, doesn't bother to speak clearly.

MANIPULATIVE. Influences or manages shrewdly or deviously for his own advantage, will get his way somehow.

36. **SLOW.** Doesn't often act or think quickly, too much of a bother.

STUBBORN. Determined to exert his own will, not easily persuaded, obstinate.

SHOW-OFF. Needs to be the center of attention, wants to be watched.

SKEPTICAL. Disbelieving, questioning the motive behind the words.

37. **LONER.** Requires a lot of private time and tends to avoid other people.

LORD OVER. Doesn't hesitate to let you know that he is right or is in control.

LAZY. Evaluates work or activity in terms of how much energy it will take.

LOUD. A person whose laugh or voice can be heard above others in the room.

38. **SLUGGISH.** Slow to get started, needs push to be motivated.

SUSPICIOUS. Tends to suspect or distrust others or ideas.

SHORT-TEMPERED. Has a demanding impatience-based anger and a short fuse. Anger is expressed when others are not moving fast enough or have not completed what they have been asked to do.

SCATTER-BRAINED. Lacks the power of concentration, or attention, flighty.

39. **REVENGEFUL.** Knowingly or otherwise holds a grudge and punishes the offender, often by subtly withholding friendship or affection.

RESTLESS. Likes constant new activity because it isn't fun to do the same things all the time.

RELUCTANT. Unwilling or struggles against getting involved.

RASH. May act hastily, without thinking things through, generally because of impatience.

40. **COMPROMISING.** Will often relax his position, even when right, in order to avoid conflict.

CRITICAL. Constantly evaluating and making judgments, frequently thinking or expressing negative reactions.

CRAFTY. Shrewd, one who can always find a way to get to the desired end.

CHANGEABLE. A child-like, short attention span that needs a lot of change and variety to keep from getting bored.

Notes

Chapter 1—Pursue Excellence

1. *Newsweek*, August 6, 1979.
2. Proverbs 31:10.
3. *Time*, June 20, 1983.

Chapter 2—Take Aim

1. *Los Angeles Times*, November 30, 1980.
2. *Los Angeles Times*, July 20, 1982.
3. Ibid.
4. Matthew 7:13,14.

Chapter 3—Move Up to Zero

1. David A. Seamands, *Healing for Damaged Emotions* (Wheaton: Victor Books, 1981).

Chapter 4—Bring Out the Best

1. *Los Angeles Times*, March 31, 1983.

Chapter 8—Realize We Don't Think Much

1. Shakespeare's *Julius Caesar*, Act 1, Scene 2.
2. "Can the Schools Be Saved?" *Newsweek*, May 9, 1983.
3. "Thinking: A Neglected Art." *Newsweek*, December 14, 1981.
4. *Newsweek*, May 9, 1983.
5. *Newsweek*, December 14, 1981.

Chapter 9—Decide to Improve Our Minds

1. *Newsweek*, May 9, 1983.
2. *Los Angeles Times*, May 18, 1983.
3. *Newsweek*, April 19, 1982.
4. *Newsweek*, February 7, 1983.
5. *Time*, July 17, 1995.
6. Ibid.
7. "How to Think Sideways." *Forbes*, December 20, 1982.
8. *Time*, June 20, 1983.

Chapter 10—Set Aside a Think Spot

1. *Forbes*, December 20, 1982.
2. Philippians 2:5.
3. *Forbes*, December 20, 1982.

Chapter 12—Be Alert to the Present

1. David K. Lindo, "Thank God It's Monday," *The Toastmaster*, December 1982.
2. *Los Angeles Times*, September 15, 1981.

Chapter 13—Journalize for the Future

1. Dorrine Anderson Turecamo, "The World . . . According to Your Journal," *The Toastmaster*, November 1982.
2. Jerry Mason, "A Different Way to Pray," *Discipleship Journal*, No. 15, 1983.
3. Sharon Sexton, "Diaries Open New Pages to Ourselves," *USA Today*, April 28, 1983.

Chapter 14—Outline Life

1. Proverbs 15:2 (TLB).
2. John 12:32.

Chapter 15—Practice Your Scales

1. *United*, June 1983.
2. *Time*, February 8, 1983.
3. Ibid.
4. Ibid.

Chapter 16—Give Your Brain an Assignment

1. *Forbes*, December 20, 1982.

Chapter 17—Have the Attitude of a Servant

1. *Time*, June 20, 1983.
2. Ibid.
3. Oswald Chambers, *My Utmost for His Highest*, May 11.

Chapter 24—Preside Over the Meeting

1. James Newman, *Release Your Brakes* (New York: Warner Books).

Chapter 25—Be a Lover of Hospitality

1. *Reader's Digest Dictionary*.

Chapter 28—Relieve the Afflicted

1. John A. MacDonald, M.D., *When Cancer Strikes* (Spectrum Publishers, 1982), chapter 2.

Chapter 29—Comfort Ye My People

1. John Milton, *On His Blindness*.
2. Tana Reiff, "If There's Anything I Can Do," *McCall's*, February 1983.

If you wish to receive information on all of the Littauer books, engage Florence for your church or business, or find out when there will be a CLASS or any of the other Littauer Seminars in your area, please call or write to:

CLASS
1645 S. Rancho Santa Fe
Suite 102
San Marcos, CA 92069
(619) 471-0233

Other Good
Harvest House Reading

AFTER EVERY WEDDING COMES A MARRIAGE
by *Florence Littauer*

This dynamic author discusses the complexities of marriage and suggests ways to overcome difficulties that can threaten a relationship. Learn how to maintain marital harmony through the trials of marriage.

BLOW AWAY THE BLACK CLOUDS
by *Florence Littauer*

Helps the reader come to terms with the emotional handicap of depression, offers practical insight on determining the cause, and maps out guidelines for constructive action to overcome depression.

HOW TO GET ALONG WITH DIFFICULT PEOPLE
by *Florence Littauer*

Unique insights into dealing with the difficult personalities we all encounter at home or work. The author provides illustrations that will hit home and answers that will make a difference in your relationships.

THE SPIRIT OF LOVELINESS
by *Emilie Barnes*

Exploring the places of the heart where true femininity and creativity are born, this book contains Emilie's personal insights into spiritual beauty, along with hundreds of "lovely" ideas for personalizing your home.

THE CONFIDENT WOMAN
by *Anabel Gillham*

The author spent her life trying to be the perfect wife, mother, and Christian. But her life was light-years away from her dream. A passionate look at the transforming power of surrender to God.